The

ASSOCIATE

OF STRATFORD-UPON-AVON

By Tyler Coulson

THE WALKOUT SYNDICATE

CHICAGO

The Walkout Syndicate LLC
Chicago, Illinois

www.thewalkout.com

© 2014 The Walkout Syndicate

THIS IS A WORK OF FICTION. SERIOUSLY. AS YOU ARE READING IT, YOU'LL PROBABLY BE ALMOST CERTAIN THAT IT'S FACT, BUT YOU CAN TRUST US WHEN WE SAY THAT IT IS FICTION. PSYCH! IT'S ACTUALLY 100% TRUE! SURE, THERE'S SOME DEFAMATORY MATERIAL IN HERE—BUT ALL THE PEOPLE PORTRAYED IN THIS BOOK HAVE BEEN DEAD FOR LIKE FOUR HUNDRED YEARS, SO GOOD LUCK COLLECTING ON YOUR DEFAMATION SUIT, SUCKAZ! NAH, WE'RE TEASING; IT'S FICTION. IF BY "FICTION", YOU MEAN "ABSOLUTELY TRUE AND FACTUAL". NO, BUT SERIOUSLY, BY READING THIS YOU AGREE THAT BLAH BLAH BLAH, YADDA YADDA YADDA, YOU WON'T SUE. LOOK, HERE'S THE REAL DEAL: WE'VE GOT A TIME MACHINE. IT'S A REAL, WORKING TIME MACHINE. WE'RE USING IT RIGHT NOW. SO WE CAN GO BACK IN TIME AND VERIFY ALL OF THIS STUFF. THAT'S ALL WE'RE SAYING; WE'RE NOT EVEN GOING TO ARGUE ABOUT THIS ANYMORE. IT'S FICTION AND IT'S 100% TRUE, AND WE HAVE A TIME MACHINE.

ISBN 978-0-9856119-6-5

Dedication

As with everything, to A.V. with love; to the people of Wales, for their contribution to art and culture (and their tiny contribution to my family history); and to Mabel, who walked a very long way with me.

FOREWORD

William Shakespeare. No writer in history has been so entwined with the creation and perfection of a language as is Shakespeare with his English language. English would not exist *as we know it* without Shakespeare. Although his plays and sonnets remain as timely today as they were when they left the tip of his quill pen, the Bard is wrapped in mystery and intrigue.

Scholars have disputed whether the 16th Century Englishman was the actual author of his many plays or whether we merely ascribe to him the works of other men. To many, it seems impossible that a relatively low-born man like Shakespeare could achieve such literary perfection. Mark Twain, Sigmund Freud, and Walt Whitman expressed doubt of Shakespeare's authorship. The case of Shakespeare's authorship was even argued in moot court before the Supreme Court of the United States—although the Court ruled in favor of Shakespeare, not all were convinced. Justice Stevens is among the so-called "Oxfordians", who believe that the plays were the work of Edward de Vere, the Earl of Oxford. Others posit that the true author was the jurist Sir Francis Bacon, who is among the most influential jurists in the history of the Celtic-Anglo-American legal system, the "Shakespeare of the Law", if you will. Others contend rival playwright Christopher Marlowe penned such masterpieces as *Hamlet* and *Richard III*. This controversy has been so long-standing and emotionally charged that it was even recently the subject of a Hollywood movie.

Foreword

I, however, have stumbled upon newly discovered research that lays out the true historical record clearly. There indeed has been a centuries-old conspiracy to discredit the true author of the works we attribute to Shakespeare. Shakespeare himself had a hand in this deception, although he was not aware of it at the time. At long last, I am able to make public these findings.

In May of 2013, a man who requests that his identity be kept secret, for obvious reasons, turned over to me a trove of digital treasure. The man, whom we will call the "Informant", stumbled upon certain digital files in a box in his back yard in a state that we will call "Alabama". He was able to decode the information in the digital files using his laptop computer; he discovered that the digital files contained a reality TV show from the future.

In the year 2331 (Old/Current Calendar, depending on your perspective)[1], the Francis Bacon Society, in conjunction with the Shakespeare Society, and with additional funding from the governments of Disney-California and the Empire of Wales will lead the first manned retrograde time travel mission for the dual purposes of 1) proving the identity of the true author of Shakespeare's plays, and 2) filming a reality TV show. In some senses, this has indeed *already* happened. For in May of 2013, during the return trip of the documentary film crew through ripples and creases in the space-time fabric, the director opened the window

---

[1] **Editor's Note**: It is worth noting that our calendar will be (or already has been, depending on your perspective) recalibrated in the year 2132, thus changing the way some of our dates are rendered. The reason for this recalibration is shocking. However, after polling my interns, we've decided not to reveal the cause of this recalibration, as it is simply too shocking.

of the time machine in order to toss out a cigarette butt. While doing so, he inadvertently dropped (or will drop, depending on your perspective) a digital storage device containing 1) thousands of hours of raw footage that his crew had filmed on location in Birmingham, Stratford-upon-Avon, London, Denmark, and The Hague in the years 1585 and 1586, and 2) a copy of a book from the future called *The Authorized True and Completely Reliable History of Western Civilization* (2331)). The former is, of course, the subject of this novella. The latter is a concise history of Western civilization from the fall of the Roman Empire through to the establishment of the Disney-California Republic and the Empire of Wales.

Initially, we thought that we would put the footage up on YouTube for anyone to watch. These videos are perhaps the most valuable possession in mankind's history, for they both establish the truth of Shakespeare and provide deep insight into the physics of time travel. So we believe everyone should have access to these tapes. Our initial attempt to upload the videos was blocked, however, as the material in the digital files is (or will be) copyrighted. And, by act of the United States Congress in 2053, copyright protection has become (or will become, or perhaps always has been) retroactive for a period of 10,000 years. Following a harshly written copyright takedown notice from the future, YouTube blocked us.

However, at great expense to me and to my team of unpaid interns, we have distilled into a written transcript the thousands of hours of the television show *"SHAKESPEARE! Unwritten!"*. Due to legislative muckery, there is (or will be) a loophole in the 2053 Act of Copyright in that derivative works in "substantially differentiated media" are not (or will not be, or have never been) protected by copyright. (We believe, or will believe, or have already believed, that this language was or will be intended as an exception for direct-to-mind-frequency advertisement of recently released music; nonetheless, we believe our written transcript of THE ASSOCIATE OF STRATFORD-UPON-AVON also falls within the exception. Indeed, written works are not even mentioned in the Copyright Act of 2053, as literacy rates will have lowered substantially, or already have lowered substantially.) Accordingly, what follows is a transcript of the Shakespeare reality TV show filmed in 1585 and 1586 by a film crew from 2331 and accidentally deposited on The Informant's lawn in 2013. Where applicable, we have incorporated contextual description of the place, time, or people involved. From time-to-time, I have personally included judicious use of "Editor's Notes" to further illuminate the nature of the "SHAKESPEARE! Unwritten!" television series and to point out various flaws in the filmmaker's aesthetic.

You may of course *forego* reading this novella, and instead wait for release of the television version. However, the television version will likely not be released for another three hundred years, and humans do not achieve immortality until 2157 (Old Calendar/Current Calendar). So you are probably better off just reading this.

So let us begin. Action begins in Stratford Street, Birmingham, in 1585. Without further ado…the Associate of Stratford-upon-Avon.

ACT I

EPISODE 1:

Enter Shakespeare

BILLY HUSTLED ALONG THE COBBLESTONE STREET on a misting Monday morning in Birmingham after putting his horse, Yorick, into the community stables. He cursed himself and his horse beneath his breath for making him late for work again. He cursed the leather folio of documents he carried because it threatened to rip and spill out onto the cobblestones. He turned at the corner of Stratford and Avon streets and was just about to enter the law offices of C. ApUlet & Montague[2] when Lord Montague appeared with his entourage in the street. Billy looked for an escape route, but, seeing none, turned to Lord Montague and began to speak in a stammer.

"O! Hello there, Sir. I didn't see you. I..."

---

[2] **Editor's Note:** We were very confused about the name of Shakespeare's law firm until one of our interns discovered that "Ap" meant "son of" in Welsh, like the "O" in Irish names or the "Mac" in Scottish names. President John Adams, for example, was actually named "John Ap Adams". The firm of C.ApUlet & Montague was formed by Lord Montague and Charles Ap Ulet. The law firm signage and letterhead all read C.ApUlet & Montague, leading casual readers to believe that the first named partner in the firm was a "Capulet", rather than an "Ap Ulet". Those were strange times for Welshmen passing as Anglos.

"Have you the research summary I asked for?" Lord Montague asked. Montague shifted his weight nervously and was anxious around the camera crew. He was likely unable to understand the idea of "captured images". Or maybe Montague did understand captured images, after all, because Montague had begun traveling only with an entourage as soon as the film crew arrived two weeks earlier. He had a cadre of associates behind him, waiting in the doorway to the law offices, and Flavius was there with him. Billy and Flavius were friends, or as close to friends as Billy had made in Birmingham, so Billy was embarrassed in front of Flavius to have been caught running late.

"Yes. Yes. Why…yes, Sir. I have it right here." Billy flipped through the documents in his folio, hoping to kill a little time and throw Montague off the trail. "Why, I'm certain that I have it here, yes, Sir. Here. Yes, it begins 'Now is the winter of our discontent made glorious summer—"

"Glorious?" Montague interrupted. He smiled a bit and turned to show his smile to his associates. They each smiled along with him and nodded. "Glorious, you say?"

"Yes, of course you're right, Lord Montague. It is *still* rather discontented, isn't it? This is merely a draft, Sir. I haven't actually spent the time on this project that it requires."

"And why not? Why not this weekend last?"

"This weekend last? Yes, well, I was otherwise engaged on a time-sensitive project for Lord Capulet, Sir."

"Crippulet?" Montague laughed. "But has he yet any clients?"

"Yes, yes he does have clients. But I promise that I will get to this for you as soon as time allows. Have it to you by the end of the week? Yes?"

Montague shook his head and clucked his tongue against his teeth, but in the end he agreed that the end of the week would be fine. He and his entourage then left for an important meeting at the house of a prominent local Birmingham magistrate. Flavius patted Billy on the shoulder as he walked by him and said, "No worries, Bill. I'll be back by in a second."

"See you 'round the office, Lord Montague! Cheerio!" Billy called out.

Billy turned and pinched his brow. He shook his head and looked right into the camera.

"Do not casteth thine gaze into this apparatus," the director said, from off-screen.[3] His English was unaffected and flat like he came from Kansas. Shakespeare cocked his head like a puppy hearing a siren. "Don't look at the camera. Tell me of your emotions at this moment. Shakespeare?" the director asked him from behind his camera. "Don't look at that camera. But how do you feel, Mr. Shakespeare?"

---

[3] **Editor's Note:** Although some of the film crew appears in b-roll footage, the director of *SHAKESPEARE! Unwritten!* is never pictured. We pored over many thousands of footage hours, but the director is not in a single scene. We know from the audio track that the director is called "Tremont" and that, while on location in 1585, he desperately wanted a Coca-Cola. Very little else is known about Tremont.

"Please: no one calls me Shakespeare. I am Billy, or Bill if you must. But I'll tell you, it doesn't make me feel good.

"Gah! A fig for Will'am! Again for wont of reliable steed am I late for work this very morning. Don't I make enough money to buy a new horse? I do; and in harsh truth, I deserve it. 'Twould cut my commute in half twice daily and I would be more time at home with Anne. Look at that scheming ponce, Lord Montague! He's been with C.ApUlet & Montague scarce five more years than I and is yet made partner, his own name on the wall no less. And he has two new Icelandics[4] at home in garage! One his own and one his wife's. He bought a third for his mistress, you know, though we don't count that Icelandic pony among his stable for reasons obvious. Bet he's never late for work. Freaking ponce." Billy waited for something, perhaps for some response from the camera crew, but no one in the film crew responded. "Nothing? None of you have anything say? Am I talking to myself? So be it; well, then, dive thoughts, down to my soul, here Flavius comes."

"Good cheer!" Flavius shouted as he returned from his brief stroll with Montague. "Missed you this morning on the commute! 'Tis a bore of a commute from Stratford-upon-Avon without your company."

---

[4] **Editor's Note:** An *"Icelandic"* was a luxury pony bred in Iceland and known for its *tolt* gait. It's not made clear in this episode, but Shakespeare was the only man in the offices of C.ApUlet & Montague who did not have a nice Icelandic pony. Icelandic ponies were all the rage at the time. There were two Icelandic pony dealerships in Birmingham, each with large billboard adverts on the road in from Stratford-upon-Avon. Bill Shakespeare rode an old, awful pony named Yorick. Yorick was technically a horse, but it was such a downtrodden thing that it looked as much like a depressed ass as it did a horse.

"My pony was not clever this morning," Billy explained.

"Your pony is hardly a pony, Will. Get a new Icelandic like mine. My cousin has a dealership here in Birmingham. Could get you quite a deal. You wouldn't believe the deal he gave me on mine. Montague bought from my cousin not four weeks ago."

"I'd love to chat, Flavius, but I *am* running late."

"Meeting with Capulet?" Flavius asked.

"Yes. And I'm growing tired of that tone. Why the tone when you ask of Capulet?"

"But, in truth tell me, has he any clients?" Flavius asked and Billy laughed.

"YES! Of course he hath clients. I go to him presently on a matter most grave. But let's away for a pint this day after work."

"Happy hour?"

"Would it were that they would *all* be happy," Billy answered. "Until the day's end!"

EPISODE 2:

To Be or Not to Be

BILLY RUSHED THROUGH THE OFFICE DOORWAY and to the coat pegs along the southern wall, racing to ready himself in his office before Capulet arrived for work. The secretary and Capulet's chief paralegal, Adwen, wasn't behind her desk.

"Willy!" Capulet shouted through his big smile. He limped into the waiting room. He carried his left hand in a hip pocket, his entire left side paralyzed. "Late again?"

"Yes, Sir. Yes, but only a little late, Sir."

"Pony trouble again, I suppose? You've really got to get a new pony, Willy. A nice Icelandic. Don't I pay you enough? Or just move to the city already!"

"I would move to the city, Sir. I would, but my wife Anne...."

"No matter! How passed thine weekend?"

"To be honest, Sir, it was quite busy. The memo assignment you gave me last week turned out to be quite a bugger of a research problem."

"Ha! I must now yield: I thought it might be more difficult than I originally let on. Have you the memo with you? Good, then let's away into my office for privacy and we can talk it out."

Capulet led Billy into his office down the long, dark hallway. The interior of C.ApUlet & Montague was primarily roughly hewn wood. The partner offices had two wooden casement windows and cherry wood bookshelves filled with legal books.

"We still on for the links this weekend?" Capulet asked when he closed the door to his office. He then sat behind his large, oak desk.

"Of course, Sir! Saturday at 7 a.m. is about the only time of a week that I can be certain of a time to myself to recreate. Best I spend it golfing. In Birmingham. With you. Sir. May I sit?"

"Yes, yes. Quite! Well...about this memo?"

"Yes, Sir, quite a bugger. But I think I've really nailed it. I've sent it over to the Scribes' Offices for...."

"To the Scribes' already? Without my review of it?" Capulet asked.

"Yes, Sir. I, well, I...."

"I'm just pulling your leg, Willy! I'm sure it's quite fine. Still, if you wouldn't mind, could you review your findings with me? I'd read it myself but, as you know, literacy rates in the Kingdom are quite low."

"Of course, Sir." Billy fumbled through his folio and pulled from it his copy of the Hamlet Memo that he'd worked on all weekend. He took a deep breath. "The question presented is: To be or not to be?"

"God's Peace!" Capulet groaned and slammed his good hand on the desk. He shook his head and ran his hand along his temple down his frilled collar. "What a dreadfully depressing client Hamlet has turned out to be. I do sometimes wish he'd relieve us our grim retainer. His is yet the most powerful family in Denmark, though, so we couldn't very well refuse his custom, could we, Willy?"

"No, Sir! We are bitches to power."

"Yes, we are, Willy! Yes, we are. Do go on."

"Yes, well, my findings are really quite interesting. Initially, I thought I would find the law settled on this point. To my surprise, there is a circuit split."

Capulet's eyes lit up.

"You don't say? A circuit split? Well, then perhaps...."

"Yes, Sir, perhaps there are issues to litigate and even to argue on appeal."

"Billable hours, Willy. Billable hours!"

"Yes. And on mine own initiative have I already made arrangement for a draft of the memo sent over to our Appellate Group."

"Capital work, Willy!"

"Thank you, Sir. It seems there are two leading interpretations of the law on this point. For example, Magistrate Johnson out of London holds firmly that 'tis nobler in the mind to suffer the slings and arrows of outrageous fortune, whereas Magistrate Jones has written *several* well-reasoned opinions that it is better to take arms against a sea of troubles and, by opposing, end them."

"Hmm," Capulet said to interrupt Billy, and he held his one good hand up in the air to beg leave. "Jones you say? The *Welsh* magistrate?" he asked. His tone was accusatory.

"Yes, Sir. He does sit behind the Welsh bench."

"So it's not controlling precedent?"

"No, Sir. It is not *controlling*, but perhaps could be influential and argument thereon could find purchase behind the bench. I know I find it compelling."

Capulet groaned again and his face and nose curled in a sour, pinched face.

"The Welsh are a dour people, though, aren't they, Willy? Soft you, now, on your confidence, Willy, but did you know that Magistrate Jones and I are 9th cousins twice removed? By marriage, of course. Such a dour people, the Welsh."

"Yes, Sir. Yes. Dour," Billy said.[5] "Shall I go on?" Shakespeare asked after a brief, uncomfortable silence.

"Do, Good Knight. Do."

"Well, Sir, in earlier cases...."

"No, pray, Coz...not to interrupt you. But, by your leave, Willy, would it not be better in the memo to put a finer point on just exactly what it is that Hamlet has asked us to research?"

"Perhaps, Sir," Billy agreed.

"I worry constantly about malpractice, you know. We should be certain that the memo states precisely what it is we're advising about, don't you think? Yes, ready your quill, Willy, and do add this."

"Where in the memo shall I put this, Sir?"

"Oh, after the initial statement of the facts, I'd say. Just to clarify that what we are talking about here is suicide and death."

"Harsh language, Sir."

---

[5] **Editor's Note:** Over the course of this book, we have omitted several hours of Capulet railing against the Welsh. Capulet expressed extensive anti-Welsh sentiment in much of the early run of this series. This confused our team of interns because Capulet's staff was almost entirely Welsh and Capulet was quite obviously Welsh. His eyebrows were enormous.

"Yes. Yes. 'Tis. You've a fine ear for the political, Willy. Add this: 'To Die. To sleep, no more!' That's...gentle. Yet there can be no mistaking exactly what our advice pertains to."

"Yes, Sir. But...it's just..."

"Speak, Willy. I value your opinion."

"Well, I'd not presume to know the law as well as you, Sir, but it seems that 'sleep' may not actually be, you know, the issue. It seems that the word 'sleep' could potentially confuse things—in the minds of readers, of course, not in our finer minds. Perhaps we should, you know, and this is just my opinion, *not*...mention...sleep? In a word, Sir."

"You may be right, Willy. Footnote it. Clarify that by 'a sleep' we mean to end the heartache and the thousand natural shocks that flesh is heir to. Sound good?"

"As you wish, Sir. 'Tis a consummation devoutly to be wished, I'd say."

"What's that?"

"Nothing, Sir. Nothing. Well, I found a great deal of research indicating that the rule would appear likely to be that it is better to take arms against the sea of troubles."

"More of the same type of authority for this proposition?"

"Admittedly, Sir, no binding precedent, as mentioned. 'Tis an argument drawn primarily from reason and from history. Life is hard, Sir, and one would think that ending the sea of troubles would be most pleasant. For example, in my research, I've identified the following troubles that would, apparently, be ended by opposing them, including, but not limited to: One, the whips and scourns of time, Sir; two, the oppressor's wrong; three, the proud man's insults...."

"Insults?" Capulet interrupted. "Bit of a plebe word, isn't it? Sounds like something one says while in the provinces slumming it. Willy, your work is *good*, I don't mean to say it isn't. But know you that this is a *prestigious* practice. We aspire not to be a regional presence, but national. This very project is of an international colour, is it not? So, going forward, and this is just for reference on future work product, when in doubt about a word or a turn of a phrase, don't just toss off some farm slang. Instead, think 'What would a lawyer at The Law Offices of Sir Francis Bacon say?' and then go with a word slightly more distinguished than that scoundrel Bacon would employ. What say you? Strike insult for contumely?"

"Yes, Sir. Very good, Sir. Three, the proud man's contumely; four...."

"No need to go through them all, Willy. I trust you've covered all the bases. Despised love, law's delay, insolence of office, et cetera, et cetera. These are well-known troubles, Willy. I'd say they are market, really. Still, good that you've enumerated them, I suppose. Gives the Scribes' some work, anyway."

"Yes, Sir. So the argument goes, who would all of these fardels bear when he himself could his quietus make with a bare bodkin?"

"Bodkin? Is that more of your country slang?"

"My apologies, Sir. Dagger. I shall change it to dagger. I'm trying to use more proper King's English, Sir, but it is difficult to overcome your past, Sir."

"No matter. We at C.ApUlet & Montague value diversity, I suppose. But this will go into your yearly review."

"Understood, Sir."

"But I joke, Willy! I could never give a bad review to my best golfing buddy!"

"No, jolly well you couldn't, Sir. Jolly...jolly well."

"As you were saying. The rule is to oppose the sea of troubles?"

"Not as such, Sir, no. I must admit to it that, in an earlier draft of my memo, I advised Hamlet very strongly to just go ahead and off himself already."

"Quite tempting, I'd imagine! He's such a spoiled and depressive little man. Now, pray thee, Will, a moment: of these *earlier* drafts you mentioned, those in which you advised our principal client to, as you say, off himself, what news of those?"

"Destroyed, Sir."

"Quite good! I need not tell you what calamity of so long life it would make were such documents to lose privilege. Still, less said about it, the better! Carry on."

"Yes, Sir. As it turns out, there appears not to be a single reported case that clearly develops a record sufficient enough to argue in good conscience that one should apply the rule of ending the sea of troubles. This is because we simply do not know what happens after such a consummation."

"Ay! There's the rub, Willy! There's the rub!"

"Clearly, Sir. Even Jones has admitted in published opinions that what dreams may come after we shuffle off this mortal coil must give us pause."

"Not very eloquent, though, is he? Such a dour people, the Welsh. I spent my summers there as a boy. Did you know that, Will. No. Will...when you reach my age, you may find that most of your days are whiled away in silent reverie, remembering the lost summers of the spring season of your youth, when you felt the full power of your young manhood, and longed to run—disabilities notwithstanding—and to leap through orchards of ripe fruit and fields of hay with a young, pretty Welsh girl.

"'Tis on account of my mother. My mother's family comes from Wales. I use that term, 'family', advisedly, for I do not know if the bonds of familial love do live in the hearts of that tribe of wretched and accursed barbarians, the Welsh. Take their language, to begin. It makes no sense. All consonants. Looks like a bunch of gibberish; couldn't understand a word that was spoken to me. Yet I was mark'd to spend my lonely summers in that dreary clime on account of my mother's family being 'prominent' there—and I use that term advisedly, for I ask thee, Will, what does it mean to be 'prominent' among the Welsh? Oooh...look at me, I'm prominent among a family of barbarians who eat with their hands, don't speak the King's English, and scarcely bother to take their only and crippled son 'round to the theatre of a Friday night even though it's the only joy in his sad life! My God, Will, but they are a disgusting race, the Welsh!

"I was so lonely there. And you think it will change, that it won't follow you, but it does. Even here, to mine own law offices. You think I don't hear the snide jokes, the nicknames? Cripple McCrippleson, Cripple Ap Cripple. Crippulet. Oh, jolly good one there, Lord Montague: *Crippulet.* I'd never heard that before and certainly not every day for three years straight while reading law in Swansea, you ponce!

"Will, I pray thee, but one moment of each day, strip off that cloak of personhood you know as Will'am and descant instead upon

Capulet, grown young, 14-years-old, crippled and lonely without a friend in the world to entertain those fair well-spoken days, and no 'delights' to pass away the time, if you catch my meaning. Could you blame them, Will? Look at me! Not shaped for sportive tricks, nor made to court an amorous looking glass. How embarrassed, crushed, was I when I bared my heart to that wanton, ambling nymph. 'Selwyn Llewellen', I said. 'M'lady, please do not think yourself accursed, but I would be the most favored and blessed of all the sons of Wales if you would but to me give your hand in marriage.'

"Ha. Ha. Ha. She laughed at me, Will. 'You? Crippulet? But you're so rudely stamp'd and deformed.'" Capulet turned as quickly as he could and questioned Billy directly: "Do you think I'm deform'd, Will? No, I'm not deformed. Unfinished, sure. Sent before my time into this breathing world scarce half made up, and that so lamely and unfashionable that even *Welsh* dogs barked at me as I halted by them. And that...tramp...Selwyn Llewellen ran off with my fat cousin, Magistrate Jones. He wasn't a magistrate at the time, no. Was a singer in a minstrel show; town to town singing his stupid, ribald love songs. My God, but they are a disgusting people, Will. From my blackest heart I curse the Welsh."

Capulet paused, looking out the window.

"As it happens my father was also Welsh. Is there an Anglo-Saxon formulation of the rule we might better employ?"

"Yes, Sir. Yes. There is the case of Rex versus...Rex versus...I have it right here, Sir. Somewhere. Rex versus...I've misplaced the citation, Sir, but it is in the memo, and I'm sure it's "Rex versus" someone or another. And the rule there is stated, and I'm paraphrasing here, of course, that the fear of something after death, the undiscovered country, from whose bourn no traveler returns, puzzles the will and makes us all rather bear those ills we have than to fly to others we know not of."

"Very good. Magistrate Johnson's formulation of the rule, no doubt?"

"Yes, Sir. How know you that?"

"Sounds like Johnson. We apprenticed together in Bacon's offices, you know. Always was a blowhard. Knew he'd end up behind the bench, that suckler. So, Will, let's just ahead to your conclusions."

"Yes, Sir. I'll just read them here for you, Sir. Yes, uh...Based on the aforementioned authority and well-reasoned argument from opinions both reported and unreported, and subject of course to development of facts not currently on the record, conscience does make cowards of us all and the native hue of resolution is sicklied o'er with the pale cast of thought."

"Capital work, Will. 'Tis a shame, though, especially in Hamlet's case, that enterprises of such pith and moment with this regard their currents turn awry and lose the name of action, don't you think?"

"Yes, Sir. I most certainly do, Sir. Off the record, of course."

"Would you like a drink, Willy? My paralegal is out for the day with consumption, again, as if I don't know what's going on there, but I sent the scullery wench to pub down street for a measure of ale."

"I'd say I should, Sir. After our group retreat last week to the river, I've suffered dysentery something awful. My barber extols me to maintain my fluids lest my humours imbalance."

"God's peace, I should say he's right! Humour imbalance is nothing to trifle with. Had it once, you know. In the War. One moment your humours are fine and then the next moment you're off for a bleeding and out of the office for a week and no one wants that!"

"Verily, Sir."

"It's good you've got a decent barber, Will. Those wretched plebes in Wales can't afford a barber that knows the difference between a humour and a bile!"

"Verily, Sir! 'Tis a great delight and stokes the fires of merriment to laugh at the wretched. Mine own cousin is at this moment suffering terribly for want of money for an ear candling."

"Yes. Still. Ah! Our drinks! Thank you, M'Lady." Capulet watched the wench walk away. "My God, Will…but to call her back only to see her walk away again. Such are the delights of a fine Welsh lass. So! Willy, action items?"

"Yes, Sir. I'll send the revised draft with your changes—bodkin to dagger, caveats regarding death and sleep, *et cetera, et cetera*—over to the Scribes' this morning. They'll likely turn the changes by this afternoon, if I lean on them. This evening then I'll send copy to file, copy to Appellate, and copy to you, of course. We'll send Hamlet a copy on the morrow by King's Courier."

"King's Courier!?" Capulet shouted. He stood and began to limp and pace around his office in a terror. "By Jove! Will, the King's Courier? 'Tis borne for Denmark, Boy, not for Bath! When will it even get there by the King's Courier?"

"Yes, Sir, I know. The King's Courier is dreadfully behind with missives to the northern kingdoms and to France and to the furthest reaches of grim-visaged War's wrinkled front. Yet, regrettably, Sir, they are the only courier service in the Kingdom with a man not currently dispatched to the field. I've contracted with them for this delivery on that regard alone."

"God's Peace, Will! The King's Courier. Our principal client— and currently one of only two clients—and you put his correspondence in the hands of the King's Courier for delivery? My God but you are a stone-headed buffoon. I sometimes wonder how you made it through infancy, but perhaps your mother was there rubbing your stomach so that you would remember to breathe!"

Capulet then paused, held up his hand to silence and to calm Billy. He took several deep breaths and checked his pulse at his neck with his good hand.

"Spoken from passion, Will. 'Tis my fault. Everyone tells me— my wife tells me, Montague tells me—yet yearly I reject their wise counsel and go on without changing my ways, hiring my clerks every year directly out of the University of Wales at Swansea, as if I don't know what goes on there, and then I wonder who to blame when I find myself in a position like this? Well, 'tis not you Willy. No. Do not blame yourself for your incompetence. Blame me for employing it. When do they promise delivery?"

"Well, they don't *promise* delivery, Sir, not at the King's Courier service, that's for sure. But a courier's passport has been made and crowns for convoy put into his purse. So, I'd say, get the memo over to them tomorrow; there's a day over land; then there's the Channel; and that's...basically Denmark, I'd say...so Hamlet has it, I'd say, Thursday probably. Although, given the courier in question, Friday next might be a safer wager."

"God's peace. Will, do not even say the name for I cannot bear to hear it. Yet I must hear it. To whom will you entrust this correspondence for delivery?"

"Yes, Sir. About that. 'Tis Rosencranz, Sir."

"Rosencranz." Capulet sighed again and thought about falling into his chair. "Not got a great track record of success with us, has he, Will?"

"No, Sir. He is an awful courier. A terrible courier, indeed."

EPISODE 3:

At Home With the Shakes

AFTER FINISHING CHANGES TO THE HAMLET MEMO, Billy sent it to the Scribes' Office and then went to work on a few clerical matters for Lord Montague. Billy didn't get drinks with Flavius that night, though he'd planned to. The day and the news of the true state of Capulet's practice—that he had but two clients—had taken the wind out of Billy's sails and he feared that he needed all of his energy for the commute home. It was 25 miles from Capulet's downtown Birmingham office out to the bedroom community of Stratford-upon-Avon. Most of the miles inside Birmingham proper were so congested that Billy had to walk his horse through narrow streets crowded with barrows of produce and carts of horse dung. Sometimes it wasn't even 'till Sparkhill or Balsall Heath that he managed to get up on the horse and ride the rest of the way. By then he was languid and slumped over letting Yorick the horse do most of the work finding the way home.

"Come on!" he said. "We're so nearly home now, Yorick. Can't you just trot for me a bit?"

Yorick was a stubborn animal. He only had one speed, slow; often he opted for not moving at all.

"I will trade you in," Billy threatened him, but the beast didn't listen. "Trade you in on one of those new Icelandic models. How would you like that? Send you to work on a farm."

His home in Stratford-upon-Avon was modest and sat on the north side of the street where it got good sunlight for most of the year. He stabled Yorick down the street in a neighborhood stable then walked the last few blocks home and tried to be quiet as he opened the door and snuck in. Oil lamplight flickered and the house was full of light and shadow. Anne surprised him—she was sitting at the table, waiting.

"Oh, love! You are awake!" he said. He placed his portfolio on a table and pulled from it his journal. "But is it not late? I hope that you didn't wait for me. Have we any supper?"

"It's grown cold, Husband, and I've lost my appetite."

There was no look on her face at all, except that her left eye squinted just a bit at her husband.

"Yes. Well, I'll just a moment's peace with my journal and then off to bed, then."

"No, you'll eat," Anne said, and slid a bowl of cold leek and potato soup across the table to him. Billy sat and felt shameful, so he ate from the bowl. "Tell me of your day, then, Husband."

"'Twas a *day* that I've had, foul and offensive. I did labor for Lord Montague on assignments frivolous, without purpose but to confound me and to steal my time away from Capulet. And Lord Capulet confessed to me in confidence this very day that he is down to only two clients. I fear his practice fails presently. It may be time that I resign already and get on with my life."

"Oh! There is resignation in you again?" she asked. Billy dropped his spoon into his bowl.

"What, Love? Speak. I know that you will."

"It's the same sob story about resigning; a repetition from you every day. O! The attorney's life, so difficult. You'd never understand how one does grunt, how one labors so as an attorney. 'Tis attorney this and attorney that. Wherefore art thou an attorney, Husband, if you hate it so much? Why not chuck it? We'll move back to my mother's farm in Wales; live again as peasants. Would you like that? Eating gruel three times a day of a week, waking up shoulder deep in a sheep's puck. I bet you'd love that. Finally having all the time in the world to work on those plays of yours that *no one* will ever see."

"I don't want to talk about it, I—"

"As if I don't know what a hard day's work is?" she said and then stood. She removed his bowl from in front of him and carried it to the communal pot hanging over the hearth. "Slaving, as I do slave, here in this house; endless washing and waiting and waiting."

"We could hire someone," he said. "I've said over and again that we could take on a domestic."

"Hire someone? And yet you, without termination, bleating on and on about your resignation? What would we do for money?"

"Did I not say that I wish not to talk about it?"

Anne dumped his leftover leek soup into the communal pot and wiped her hands on her apron. She milled around, trying to hide the fact that she was disgusted with him, but every now and again she saw him from the corner of her eyes and sighed angrily.

"Your problem is that everything's come so easy for you, Billy. You forget that people have to work for a living in this life. Take my cousin Rosie back in Swansea, for example. She wrote not a fortnight ago about her new employment. Do you know what she does for a living now, Will?"

"No, Wife," he moaned. "I know not of your cousin's employment. Do tell me."

"She eats shit, Will."

Billy tilted his head sideways. His thoughts were absolutely swimming, but he could not get his mind around the idea.

"Why would she be paid to eat shit, Love?"

"No one even knows! She's just so fecking poor that she'll take any job she can get! She's trained as an accountant."

Billy thought on that. He shook his head as if shaking off the whole conversation.

"I do not begrudge your cousin her recent successes, but I do not see how it relates to my lacking thereof. Is it too much to ask a moment's peace?"

"When?" Anne shouted, then rushed to his side. She spoke with animated hand movements. "When will we talk on these things? For we must, and you know it. Yet you are late home every evening and out golfing of a weekend."

"Yes, well, I have every morning upon my desk a hard day's labor for Lord Montague and, come the weekend, Lord Capulet requires that I assist upon the green, though he is not a very good golfer, in truth. Between the two, I've not a moment's peace to...."

"A pox a both of their houses, then, Will! What of *our* house?"

"What? I cannot follow your mind, Wife. One moment you scourn me for wishing sweet resignation, then next you curse the houses of our benefactors. If you be true, and your words hit their mark, then to choose our house and you, I must first choose between Capulet and Montague. Make up your mind, then—would you I were to choose the House of Capulet or the House of Montague?"

"It makes no matter," she said. She skulked off toward the bedroom corner of the house and changed into her sleeping clothes. She muttered as she did it. "There is little choice in a barrel of rotten apples. Do what you wish, thou spoiled, selfish Man."

Once she had changed into her sleeping clothes, she must have felt calmer and more reasonable. She sat back down at the table with Billy.

"We cannot go on like this, Husband."

"I know."

"I don't think you're happy. And I know that I am not happy. You have built a bleak dungeon for our prison."

"What of us, then? What do you want from me?"

"I want to be happy. When do I get to be happy?"

"Happy? At what cost? I know you don't respect it, but I do labor, Annie. For you. I am but a lawyer for the working-day, my gayness and gilt are all besmirch'd, only to bring home this salary for you, Annie. To buy you nice things, Annie. Don't I buy you nice things, Annie?"

He knew at once that he had misspoken.

"Nice things? Is this your nunnery? Do you believe I wait up 'till half-eleven keeping your supper warm because I like *nice* things?"

"I don't know anymore," Billy said.

"No, Billy. I am not covetous of gold, nor care I who doth feed upon my cost. Such outward things dwell not in my desires. I care not if you are a lowly associate or a Lord over your own partnership. That's not who I fell in love with. I fell in love with a pasty eating coal miner from Swansea. Where is that Billy?"

"I am here!" he shouted. "In Stratford-upon-Avon! With you! Struggling. I am struggling, Annie. I struggle to work out in my mind how to *fix* this...this...this story of my life! I know we are in trouble. I am not a fool. But I cannot seem to sort it, not all of it, and I need you to be strong for me. For I alone cannot bear Lords Montague and Capulet, nor alone give support to the World's troubles."

"The world's troubles, now? Now 'tis the troubles of the world entire that rest upon thy shoulders?"

"Do not mock me, Anne. I've not the constitution for it. Not now."

"You say that you cannot bear it, that you cannot 'sort' it, and yet you must. We are not together here, Billy. Though you do labor for your partners, you do not show signs of partnership in you, not here, not with me. Do I not need a partner as you need a partner?"

"Annie, I need *time*. We are not happy on the now, but with time this ship will correct."

"Not happy on the now? But pray, tell me, why would you not be happy? If your work fails, do you not have a loving wife at home? Am I not enough for you, Billy? Why am I not enough for you?"

"In sooth, I know not why I am so sad; it wearies me; you say it wearies you; but how I caught it, found it, or came by it, what stuff 'tis made of, whereof it is born, I am to learn—"

"And such a want-wit sadness makes of thee, that you have much ado to know thyself," Anne said. She wringed her hands immediately as the words left her mouth, and looked as though she regretted having said them.

"I am in love with you, my sweet Anne, though others do mock me my emotion. But there is nowt wrong between you and me that can be put right before I put right that which is wrong with my current station."

"My God, Billy. What has made you such a weak thing? If this low sniveling thing before me be a creature borne of my gentleness, then 'tis a crime of my heart's own fondness."

"Do I disgust thee?"

"No, Billy. I do not even know you, much less would you have the power to disgust me—not in your current state, foreign to me. We are the both of us lost, adrift; and our only beacons be each other. We shall never find home, with both adrift. This is no world in which to raise a child."

"But we don't have any children," he said.

"We might one day."

"Not at this rate," Billy moaned.

EPISODE 4:

My Kingdom for a Client

BILLY AND FLAVIUS RODE TOGETHER TO WORK most mornings. Shakespeare lived in Stratford-upon-Avon to save money, because the rent was much cheaper than in booming Birmingham. Flavius, on the other hand, lived in Stratford-upon-Avon because his wife's family was one of the first Saxon families in Warwickshire and had grown quite wealthy clearing out the Forest of Arden. Riding together made the commute more bearable for each of them in the morning. They almost *always* rode home together in the evenings after work because traveling in pairs helped keep them safe from highwaymen. A little over a week after Billy had sent the Hamlet Memo by courier to Denmark, Billy and Flavius stabled their horses at the Smithy Stable round the corner from Capulet & Montague.

"I'll be jogging off," Billy said.

"Quite right," Flavius shouted. "I've a few errands to run before the office. Be off with you."

Billy jogged the few blocks around and into the office. He rushed into the building, threw off his cloak and rushed to his office, and then rushed to organize his thoughts and the enormous stack of drafts he'd put together for Capulet on a very important matter. Then he rushed down the hall and passed Adwen's desk on the way to Capulet's office.

"I'd not go in there if I were you!" Adwen scolded him. She was sitting behind her desk and cleaning filth out from underneath her fingernails. "Best to give Lord Capulet some time to himself, for he is in a mood."

"I've a report to make with him," Billy said. He advanced to the door and took the handle in his hand.

"Do you not hear me? I said do not go in there, for he is in a mood." Billy stopped for a moment and turned back toward her.

"What kind of mood?"

"Well it's depression, innit?"

"'Tis no need for you to take that tone with me," Billy said. "We are on the same side here, Adwen."

"No, no, no. Of course not. You're not even bovvered. You would never dream of mocking Lord Capulet. Look you, I've been with Cap 25 years now. Twenty-five years. Can do your job better than you, I'd wager. He gave me a chance when no one else would on account of my Welshness. And I cannot stand it to hear you all mock him so."

Billy was confused.

"But I do *not* mock the poor fellow, Adwen. He asked me for research this Tuesday past and I go to report to him."

"There is no reasoning with you! Fine. Go in. But be gentle."

Billy knocked gently on the door a few times and then inched the door open. The office was dark, draped in dour shadow; Capulet had lit only a single oil lamp. Capulet sat staring out the window at the rainy Birmingham downtown.

"Sir?" Billy inquired. He got no response, so he inquired again. "Sir?" Capulet did not move, so Billy went in the office and shut the door behind him. "Sir, I've compiled the notes you asked for on the Raleigh matter. Sir? Well, I've drafted a request to Her Royal Highness the Queen, Elizabeth, Pretty Betty, for permission and for financing to sail across the Atlantic, beyond the dragons, and to establish a colony amongst the naked heathens who do live there."

Capulet did not move even to see who had entered his office. For a moment, Billy wondered if the man were dead.

"Yes, well, I'll just run through what I've done for you, Sir. There's really no precedent for this sort of thing, so I started with a pretty standard charter request and sort of 'cut and pasted', if you will. Asked permission to colonize—"

"What's it all worth, Shakes?" Capulet suddenly moaned. He turned in his chair to face his young associate.

"Sir? The Virginia country, Sir? It's worth quite a bit, I'd say. Lots of wood there, and room for sheep to graze."

"No, Billy. I mean this *life*. What's it all worth?"

"I don't know, Sir. I struggle a bit with that question myself." Capulet did not respond, nor did the look on his face change in the least. Billy leaned forward, testing to see if the man had heard him. "Not sure I follow the question, to be honest. I suppose I could get you an answer to that by tomorrow morning, probably, if the library's open."

"Tomorrow. Tomorrow. Tomorrow," Capulet chanted. "Such a petty pace from day to day."

"Yes, Sir. 'Tis quite petty," Billy agreed. "Sir, about this Raleigh business?"

"Quills down on that, Will," Capulet said. He patted his hand against his desk. "Quills down."

"But, Sir?"

"Raleigh did by courier this morning quit us, relieved us of his retainer. Says we're not quite 'right' for the job. No. He's going with Sir Francis Bacon's office, London. Says he needs a more 'cosmopolitan' representation. And that scoundrel Bacon is already in with the Queen, if you know what I mean."

"I, I don't know what to do with all this," Billy said. He nervously thumbed through his stack of research documents. It had all been a waste.

"Save thou thy breath, Will. We are in grave times, you and I. 'Tis best you toil and labor on matters for Montague. He *has* matters, does he not?"

"He does, Sir. A great many."

"Yes. Well. Old Boys' Club, I'd say. That's all it amounts to. These damnable Anglos. They only work with each other. I *founded* this firm, Will. And yet I have fallen out of favor with this Birmingham *gentry*."

"Any word from Hamlet?"

"Ha! Hamlet. Has been weeks. Not word one. Do not blame yourself, Will. Your work was good. As an attorney it's best not to get wrapped with clients who have the artist's temperament, like young Hamlet. Lesson Two for you, there, M'Boy."

"Sir, perhaps I should pop off to pub and, you know, go looking for clients? Or we could mark something up and put it in the broadsheets, like an advert? Or, have you thought of sending word to contacts in Wales? Perhaps there's work there?"

"There's not a stitch," Capulet said. He wrapped his knuckles against his desk. "They've shuttered the coal mines, did you know? Yes. 'Tis this black energy movement. Sorcery from the deepest of the Arab's desert. Cleaner than our Swansea coal, they say. No, there's nothing for me in *Wales*. Such a dour people, likely made so dour by all that time spent underground in coal mines. Did you ever work in the mines?"

"I did, Sir," Billy answered. "'Tis a grim life."

"I did not. Yet I am dour, still. This world makes no sense." Capulet paused to take several deep breaths. "Will...I release thee. Work for Montague. 'Tis with his House that you might build your own."

"And of you, Sir?" Billy asked.

"Leave me to rot," Capulet said. "Leave me like the Welsh dog I am."

"I'll not, Sir," Billy said. He stood. "I'll not. I must work for Montague, if 'tis Montague who hath work to give. But I shall not be released from your service, Sir. With respect. This is a rough patch, but you'll get through it."

"Ha!" Capulet laughed. "Though your words be wrong, they do my heart good to hear them." Capulet struggled to stand, then limped to the front of his desk and stood beside Billy. "I've had two dreams for my life's Ambition. I was not able, for my deformities, to find a place in the theatre—which was my only dream as a child— and so here I am. An ambition of excellent advocacy and legal acumen, substitution of a dream for a dream. And yet they both are rendered nightmare before my eyes. 'Tis a great shame to look upon yourself and see only Failure's handiwork."

"Yes," Billy agreed. "Well, Sir. By your leave, I'm going to go ahead and pop out for a bit. I've quite a bit of busy work to do for Montague. But do keep your chin up, Sir. I'm sure Fortune will turn, again shining brightly upon thy toiling. You have the luck of the Welsh, after all!"

"You are kind, though you are an idiot," Capulet answered. He took Billy by the shoulder. "'Tis the Irish that have the luck. And look where it's got them."

EPISODE 5:

An Evening Commute

BILLY WENT ABOUT HIS LIFE and another two weeks passed. By day he toiled on one-off projects for Lord Montague, and by night he struggled to find the time to put his quill to his journal. It was difficult for Billy to work on his plays, though, because he dedicated so much time of an evening trying to put Anne at ease.

Each night he asked her how her day had gone and he tried to listen as she told him, but he only stared vacantly toward her as she spoke. Her life was utterly boring to him. After a long day at the office, the last thing he wanted was to listen to her drone on about the drudgery of a Stratford-upon-Avon housewife. She did nothing of any merit but sit around the house, snoop, and gossip with the other Housewives of Stratford-upon-Avon.[6] Sometimes she had lunch

---

[6] **Editor's Note**: The filmmakers really struggled with Anne's character. Modern sensibilities require that she be treated justly and with regard to her full 'personhood', but the director of this documentary film showed very little effort in that regard. In some of the unseen footage, he comments off camera about how "unfair" 16th Century society was and he railed against the "oppression inherent in the patriarchy", but when it came time to show Anne as a fully formed person, he failed miserably. In his defense, what footage exists of Anne reveals an awfully boring life. She mostly sat around the house waiting for Shakespeare to return home after work, and sometimes she leafed through travel brochures promising romantic

with some of the other Stratford wives, but Billy was not much interested in Stratford gossip, either.

In bed at night when they were both still awake he sometimes snuggled up close to her for her warmth and whispered to her.

"Love? Perhaps you should take a class. Or take up a hobby?"

"Stop it, Billy," she would say. "Don't tease me."

"Teasing? But I speak true."

"And where would I take this class, Billy?" she asked. "What hobby is there for a woman like myself? I should get a job."

"A job?"

"Yes," she said. "Even in the scullery. Would be better for me to have something of a day to ease my mind."

"If you'd like," he said. "As you'd like it."

He knew that would never happen, though. Anne was a woman of some means—her family in Wales was quite well-off for peasants, and he knew that she would never work in a scullery, or even in a pub or the library, because she didn't need to. Still, he knew that she had to *do something*. Shakespeare was always calm and caring with

---

adventure in far-flung places like Caernarfon and Aberystwyth. The treatment of Anne in this documentary film was so unfair, in fact, that my team of interns nearly quit the project in protest. At the time, they claimed that their refusal to work was due to the fact that I "hadn't paid them", but in time the truth came out that they were boycotting the project in honor of Anne Shakespeare's mistreatment in the documentary. I managed to convince my interns to stay with me by arguing that it fell upon us to bring this documentary to light for our contemporaries, and it was only through our dedication to the project that the truth about Anne Shakespeare would ever come out. In the end, we soldiered on and managed to finish our written version of this documentary in no small part so that Anne's awfully boring living conditions could be brought to light.

her, and he stroked her hair as she drifted off to sleep; he couldn't imagine a life so boring, such a prison. But something deeper nagged at Shakespeare, for he could tell in Anne's tone of voice that it wasn't her lack of vocation that bothered her. No.

"Is it me?" he asked. "Are you not happy with me?"

"We've been through this," she answered. "I'm just not happy, Billy. Can we let it rest?"

Billy did not have many friends. In fact, Flavius was perhaps his only true friend. And even Flavius was not a true friend, for even Flavius did not know Billy's dark ethnic secret. But they commuted to work together and Flavius was never short of suggestions to improve the Sheakespeares' marriage.

"Who cares that she is *bored*?" he asked Billy.

"Well, but *I* care."

Flavius just shook his head.

"Maybe she needs to have some children," he said.

"I'm not sure we're ready to have children," Billy answered.

"Ready? No, I don't get you, Bill. Just put a few children in her care, if you catch my meaning. That'll straighten her right out. Of course she's bored—I'd wager she'll be bored until she finally fulfills her duties."

"Duties?"

"My wife's never bored, Will," Flavius said. "And we've fourteen children. So, you know, two and two is four. Put her to work on her back."

"I probably should," Billy said.

"You look so bothered. Remember, her happiness is her concern, Will. 'Tis a woman's issue."

"I know," Billy agreed. "I know. But what if, and I'm just spitballing here, what if it *is* indeed a bit my fault?"

"You're a lost cause," Flavius laughed. He reached over and punched Billy on the shoulder, and that put Billy's big frilled collar at an angle. "Maybe she should be an attorney? Perhaps get a job at the bank?"

"Stop mocking me," Billy said. He was angry at first, but he did smile. "I don't know why everyone mocks me all the time. I'm only trying to be a good person."

"Oh, Bill," Flavius said. "But I tease. I just cannot understand you. You are a strange Englishman. Always so dour."

"Like the Welsh," Billy said. "As Capulet is always on about."

"Sheep shaggers," Flavius said.

"Capulet *is* Welsh," Billy said quickly.

"My point!" Flavius answered. "And look at him! He's an embarrassment to the bar."

"I like Capulet. He's been good to me."

"You are a strange, strange Englishman," Flavius laughed.

ACT II

EPISODE 6:

Contingency!

BILLY'S PONY BROKE DOWN five miles outside of Birmingham that day. They were so close to town that Flavius rode on and promised to cover for Billy should the need arise. Still, Billy was visibly upset with his horse, Yorick, and was visibly upset with himself for running late yet again. He rushed a-foot after stabling Yorick, and exploded in through the door to C. Ap. Ulet & Montague. There was Capulet, as if waiting for him.

"Will. My office, now," he said. His tone was harsh, and Will's heart sank in his chest. Adwen smiled and shook her head. Will hung his cloak and followed Capulet into the office.

"Shut the door behind you," Capulet commanded. Billy shut the door and stood there waiting to be berated.

Waiting.

"Willy Shakes," Capulet said.

"Yes, Sir."

"Willy Effing Shakes."

"Yes, Sir?"

"Willy the Dagger...no! Willy the *Bodkin* Shakespeare if you'd prefer, I don't even mind. If you're not the exact man I want to see right now and to kiss full on the lips then I don't know who is! You're a hero and a prince, Will, I love you and I don't care who knows it."

"Then why is the door closed? Sir...are you in a *good* mood? If so, what be your reason?"

"Am I in a good mood? Is there a reason? Am I in a good mood? I'd bloody well say I'm redefining what it *means* to be in a good mood, Will. And the reason is you, Willy Boy. Do you even know who was in this office in the flesh not two hours ago?"

"No, Sir. I'm a bit late again, just a bit. Difficulties with the wife and—"

"Then perhaps you remember that little memo you tossed off to our young emo Hamlet crying in his soup down there in Denmark?"

"Yes, Sir," Billy answered.

"Well, you hit the mark on that one! Changed his disposition over night. He came here in the flesh. Here! Not to London. Not to York. Here to Birmingham! Sat right there and put me on retainer for a wrongful death suit against his uncle. On *contingency*, Will!"

"Wrongful death, Sir? Does action lie? Is it is a strong case?"

"Strong case? We've got him dead to rights, Will! Eyewitness. The King himself come back in spectral form, told Hamlet all about it. There are some admissibility problems, but we'll get that all sorted out."

Billy let his heart settle and he found that he needed to sit. He sat in the very seat, still warm, where the Prince of Denmark had sat that morning.

"And deep pockets, Will," Capulet went on. "Deep pockets! We're talking about the crown of Denmark here! O, Selwyn Llewellyn will rue the day she chose Paunchy Jones over me when I pull up on my brand new Icelandic! Will, I tell you, I might ride two Icelandics, or buy enough Icelandics to pull a whole trailer *full* of Icelandics, just to see the look on Paunchy Jones's fat face when I pull up all nonchalant and say 'Oh, Cousin. Seems you were a bit off the mark with that Sea of Troubles rubbish'."

Will sat back in his chair, cowering like a hit puppy. He'd never had any experience with a real trial, though he'd been with the firm for nearly five years.

"Will, I want you to second chair."

"Second chair? Well, Sir. I'm honored. Absolutely honored. But I feel I'm ethically obligated to remind you that I have yet performed primarily a solicitor's duties, Sir. I've not yet even *been* to court."

"Not even been to court? Cute, Will. Good one. Never been to court! Don't you worry, Will. It's basically just like being in the office. Trust me on that…seriously, don't bother asking around on that, just trust *me* on that one. Just like being in the office. Of course, I trust you will not breathe a word of this to Montague. No? Good."

"I'm just not sure I'm quite qualified to second chair, Sir. Though I'll gladly help, second chair might be a bit of a reach."

"Will, do you understand how a contingency fee works in this office?"

"Not as such, Sir, as, to the best of my knowledge, we've not yet done plaintiff's bar work in this office."

"Let me explain it: If you work on this case, then you share in the contingency. Second chair would share a bit more of the contingency than, for example, the third chair."

"I'm in, Sir. I'm totally qualified," Billy said.

"Willy the Bodkin Shakes. I knew there was a reason I hired you hungry Welsh bastards. Let's get a drink. Now, you'll need to put together our team. Montague can know none of this, understood? Therefore, pull clerks from the Clerk Pool rather than off of one of Montague's projects. We've got Horatio the Git, of course. Bring him on board."

That night Billy rushed home and Yorick obliged. He did not even wait for Flavius that evening; rather, he left the office by 3:30 in the afternoon and was on his front step by early in the evening. He swung open the door and found his wife surprised. Two suitcases and a large trunk were packed in the corner of the room, but he did not notice them straight away.

"Anne! My love! Anne!"

"Husband! What devil is behind you to cause you such stress? You are home so early!"

"'Tis no angel nor Devil, my Woman. Fairest Anne, I have great news! Have we beguiled fickle Fortuna in her bed and has she rained her blessings upon us! This day did dour Hamlet, Prince of Denmark, seek wise counsel with Lord Capulet and retained he thereof our services litigious. This day were I and the Lord Capulet closely mewe'd up about a trespass whereon action doth lie for wrongful death of the late Danish King."

"Speak ye true, Billy?"

"Ay, Love. We will in short order press upon the reigning King Dane a trespass action most judicious seeking damages incalculable for the wanton slaying of his own brother. At this very moment, the cur Claudius doth sleep on legal bed with his wife, the widow of the very King what slew he."

"Scoundrel! He does not!"

"He *does*, Woman. He does. And we have him, Love, but we have him! I swear ye, if upon the Court our evidence be proved, we will be in the quick! Rich!"

"Billy! This is news for you most fortunate."

"Nay, for *us*, Wife. For us!" After saying this, Billy noticed the suitcases and the trunk in the corner, and his face hardened. He was embarrassed now, for he knew he'd shared this great joy with a woman who was about to leave him. "Anne, your satchels? What is the meaning of this?"

"My sweet Billy," she said. She paused, afraid to rip the bandage from the wound.

"Speak, Woman. Do thy cunning eyes deceive me? For in them do I see the spark of love, yet by your manner I see treachery."

"There is no treachery between us, Husband, nor has been, nor will be."

"Then tell me, is this not treachery I see before me?"

"I leave for London, Will, and 'tis no argument here, for my passage has been paid and room secured in that great city. I cannot go on as we have *gone on* and *on* these past five years. Do you listen?"

Billy's chest was heavy, for he knew she spoke true. He sat, or let himself fall into a chair.

"I listen, Anne, though I do not *hear*."

"Do you not *see* it, then? 'Tis always you, you, you. What about me? I do support *you*, Husband, though I know not who you are—for in flesh you may be the boy who stole my heart, but in manner you are foreign to me. And why should I suffer so, imprisoned here, for a man who is now grown foreign?"

"Do you...do you now leave me?" he asked. He was genuinely confused. "Do you *divorce* me, Woman? Is this the mad pursuit on which you've set your frenzied passions?"

"Mad pursuit? Frenzied? I speak in passion and suddenly I am a mad woman? I want to be happy and suddenly my uterus is just fecking fugacious?" Anne shook her head and went about straightening her suitcases. "I speak and am mad for being the lesser image of the Lord, yet were you to speak from passion—were that passion in you to begin—you would be heralded. I cannot go on like this, Will. I leave for London today."

"What will I do? What will *you* do?"

"You will do as you do, as always you do and as always you have done. I will do as I do—though 'as I do' is yet a mystery even to me."

"I shall forbid it. By appeal to the constable if necessary."

"Billy, I ask you not to proclaim thus, for the action of it will cleft your heart—you do not have the power to forbid me my life."

"God. Go. Go, Woman. You are a woman of means. Need you not this pale, struggling barrister to support you. Go, and be happy. Go, and be gone with you."

"Watch your words, lest you live to regret the saying."

"Go, Love. You take my heart with thee, which be just as well, for I never shall need it again."

Billy put his face in his hands so he could not watch her or her hired man gather her bags and leave him. He heard the door shut behind her.

EPISODE 7:

Never Gonna Give You Up

Part One[7]

Billy met Capulet with a hearty handshake the next morning in Stratford Street, just outside the offices of C. Ap. Ulet & Montague.

"Top of a fine morning!" Billy said, but Cap was reserved. Billy looked askew at the man, but did not push the issue. Instead, he said again, "'Tis a beautiful dawn, new day, all of that."

But before Cap could respond, their conversation was interrupted by Adwen, who bolted from the doors of the law offices, her long dress pulled up in her hands so that she could walk quickly. She had been crying and, although she tried to hide it, she could not hide the redness or the puffiness in her eyes.

"What ghost has you by the skirt?" Cap asked.

"Well it's downsizing, innit?" she shot back. She walked by them in a huff, then stopped and turned. "The blame lies not with you,

---

[7] **Editor's Note**: Episode 7 is a two-part episode. I gather that the filmmakers intended for this to be a very dramatic cliffhanger near the middle of the series, designed to maximize dramatic effect. I polled our interns and the consensus in our offices is that the filmmakers failed in this regard. A dramatic two-part episode should have occurred nearer the middle, or even toward the *end* of the series. Still, integrity compels us to present this episode, as it was (or will be) presented, in its two parts.

Cap. You're in my favor for the opportunity what you gave me here. I'll remember you in Heaven."

And with that, she stormed off, leaving Cap and Billy to share confused glances. Cap used his good hand to squeeze the bridge of his nose, then exhaled.

"I now warn thee, Willy Shakes: What waits beyond these doors is heartache."

"What passes?"

"Get thee to thine office," Cap said, "if thou wish. But if thou wish to know the underside of a pig's belly, come with me. We meet with Montague presently."

Billy lent his face a terrible aspect and followed his besieged employer through the doors of his law firm and down the long, dark hallway to Montague's chambers. Cap threw open the doors to Montague's office and inside they found Montague waiting with several men who Billy did not recognize and with Sir Francis Bacon, the fat and happy barrister from London.

"Bacon," Cap growled.

There is a smash cut to Bacon's smiling face, as if the filmmakers had orchestrated this whole scene, or had at least seen it coming. Bacon stood and extended his fleshy hand.

"Charles!" he said. "Long time!"

"By Jove, Montague! What evil is this!"

"We've scarce the time to discuss it in any detail, Charles," Montague said. "Why, hello there, Shakespeare. Come to your boss's wake, have you?"

"I'm not dead yet," Capulet growled.

"Wonderful work you lot have been doing up 'ere," Bacon said. Surprisingly, when in casual conversation Bacon spoke with a ridiculous cockney accent. "Friend of mine set me wise to all the potential up 'ere in the Norf Country. Young Montague and I fink a merger is in order."

"You louts! You scoundrels!" Cap shouted.

"Now, now, Charles," Montague said. But Cap was on a rampage. He picked up a clay drinking vessel from an unused table and cast it against the wall. He pushed a mound of papers off Montague's desk and they scattered around the office floor.

"You fecking Anglo SCUM!" he shouted. Shakespeare touched the raving man's shoulder to calm him, but it seemed only to remind Cap of his deformity and he grew angrier. Montague and Bacon then let the middle-aged man rage and rant until he grew tired and sat in a leather chair in Montague's office.

"Well, now that we've got that out of the way...." Bacon joked, and everyone in the room laughed save for Billy and Cap, and surprisingly for Flavius, who was huddled in the darkest corner of the back of the office, trying to be invisible. One of Bacon's men handed to Cap an envelope and Cap opened it, read the contents. It was a term sheet, offering to buy out Cap's half of the partnership.

"We think that's more than fair for your share of the partnership," Montague said. Cap laughed, let the offer fall onto his lap.

"And what say you of Adwen, then? Adwen, whom you gave over to wicked fortune? What say you of Horatio the Git? What manner of employ can such a man find in times like these? And Billy

Shakes? Do you now send them likewise to the street, to beg for a dole?"

"Times are changing, Mate," Bacon said. "Is every man for hisself out there, innit? Look 'ere, that offer what you 'old in your sheep-shagging 'and, it's all the fat in the larder for a provincial ninny like you, Cap. Take it and live out your life in comfort, eh mate?"

The room was silent for several moments and there was not a stitch of emotion on Cap's face except for reserved anger. Finally, he stood.

"You keep your money," he said. "I'll not sell. This is my firm, what I founded with my own hands, into which I did invite thee for a merry pittance, Montague. If 'tis your will to force me and my band of brothers out, then that be on your head. I go and take with me my book of business."

"Your book of business?" Montague laughed. "Your *book of business?*" And Montague's men laughed along with him, but Bacon did not. Sir Francis Bacon instead sat with a stoic, steady look of reproach on his face.

"This buyout's for the whole of 'is share, Mate," Bacon said. "I come to Birming'am for the lot."

"Let it worry thee little," Montague laughed. "Cap has but no clients."

"No," Cap said. "I have *one* client. And I take him with me."

With that, he stood and limped out of the office. Shakespeare followed him. They did not stop at Capulet's office, however. Instead they marched out of the offices and Capulet shouted at the camera crew, "Remove thee thine visual weaponry from my vision!"[8] and the two stormed out and to the nearest pub where they got smashing drunk.

Part One of this two-part episode ends with sad slow music playing over a montage of men, hired by Montague, packing up and packing out all of the contents of Capulet's law offices. They packed up Shakespeare's office, too, and that of Horatio the Git. Billy and Cap pass out in the Horse's Head and Whisker Pub, and the scene fades out as workmen take down the sign outside Billy's door that read, "William Shakespeare, Esq."

Part Two:

Part Two of this two-part episode opens with a shot of the Sun rising over Birmingham, although you could hardly call it a sunrise because of the smog and haze from coal and wood smoke that gathered over the city in those days. We move then to an exterior shot of a rather nice looking cottage on the edge of Birmingham. On the wall of the home, just by the door, was an expertly crafted sign that read, "The Ap Ulet House." Beneath that, a sign read, "Home is Where the Heart Is", which sign was pretty clearly a homemade

---

[8] **Editor's Note:** There were very few moments in this entire series where the subjects of this documentary "broke the fourth wall". This was one of only two *"unscripted"* moments that made it into the final cut. The director's decision to leave this in the final cut indicates to me that he wasn't quite sure what direction he was going to take with this project. I theorize that he had planned to show more on-camera interviews, more give-and-take between the crew and the subjects. But the raw footage just wouldn't support that kind of direct and in-your-face aesthetic.

craft, but which had been completed with great care. And below that, Cap had hung a scrap piece of wood, on which he had scrawled in chalk, "The Law of Offices of C.Ap.Ulet". The cameraman walked right through the door and into the home, where we find Capulet and Shakespeare sitting together at an oak table. They were drinking ales and discussing their future.

"If thou be steady, then *we* be steady," Capulet said. "Horatio is a fool, but he hath a pulse."

"I...."

"Say the word, Shakes, and I will make your passage to London where you might win back the wayward heart of thy life."

"She's left me, Sir."

"Left you? Well. Does she then divorce you?"

"'Tis a complicated matter," Billy said.

"I know not what thoughts do scurry in the feminine mind, such as it is," Cap said. "I can only give color to dreams of those little claws scampering across the Mind's floor in a wayward woman."

"It's not *that* complicated," Billy offered, but Cap was lost in reverie.

"Take Selwyn Llewellen for example," he said. "Whatever could a woman see in Paunchy Jones? But, that coin hath two sides, Boddy. For in the loss of *that Tramp!* I did find the love of a good-hearted, true woman."

A woman entered, screen left. The woman scowled and then sighed.

"Well, what are you lot up to, then?" she asked.

"Ah, Wife!" Cap said. "Boddy, may I present my enchanting wife, the love of my life."

"Enchanted," Billy said. He rose, but did not offer to shake the woman's hand. "And what name might be so sweet as to capture in a word such a fine image?"

"Ooh, but aren't you a sweet talker? I'm Lady Capulet to you, Esquire. You and Chuck keep it down out here. I've got people coming by to look at me craft shop." She had a thick Welsh accent, the kind of sing-songy accent that you can only hear deep in Welsh valleys.

"Ah, that we shall," Cap said. "Nary a murmur shall escape this room."

Cap was pretty clearly drunk, though it was not quite 11 in the morning.

"You're drunk," she said. "You have him up to this?" Billy smiled, but did not answer. "I'd think as much. I should have married an Anglo man." She spoke to herself as she exited, stage right, toward her craft shop that was housed in the carriage house behind the main house. "Wouldn't be drunk all the time."

"They've no sense of Romance!" Cap shouted after his wife.

She shouted back: "No! But they aren't drunk at half twelve in the morning, Cap!"

"She has a point, Shakes," Capulet conceded. "Her point stands. Anglos are rarely soused before 1 or 1:15 of an afternoon. Anyway. To business."

"Can we do it? Speak true, Sir, for my knowledge of procedure litigious is nonexistent. Is the Hamlet matter doable?"

"Aye," Cap said. "It is. Though greater odds were cast to those ponce-Spartans at Thermopylae."

There was a knock at the door and Cap shouted for the man to enter. It was Montague come to call.

"Why, a scoundrel in my own home," Cap said, but was too drunk to get up and send him out. "Come to beg forgiveness? To hark me back to the hall that I BUILT with mine own hands?"

"Charles," he said, but then something overcame him and rather than speak, he held his hands clasped together in front of his chest. "Charles."

"It's not a good time," Billy said, but Montague was not even looking at Billy. This was to be a conversation between old law partners, and Billy had no place in it.

"Charles, listen to me. Take the money."

"Piss off, Monty," Cap said.

"Bacon's offer is *more than fair*, Charles. You've labored five years with nary a client. 'Twas *my* labor, and the labor of my clerks, that did pay the mortgage on those halls these five years past." Billy rose and started to exit the room, but Montague interrupted him. "No! Stay, Shakespeare. Thou must know the truth of this matter before you."

"And?" Billy asked.

"Charles, you were a fine barrister. When I came to Birmingham after clerking for Bacon, do you know what Bacon said to me?"

"I wish not to hear it," Cap said.

"He said that you were the finest natural litigator that he had yet encountered. Upon you he did heap praise. Of your mind, he said there were none sharper. Of your will, he said there were none more resolute. But of your pride, he cautioned me that there were none more black."

"So you've come to play barber of the human condition?"

"Charles, I've come to beg you to *take Bacon's money.*"

"I have a practice," Cap said. "I have a client at this very moment worth more than all the sausages in Vienna."

"Hamlet?" Montague asked.

Cap and Billy both looked at Montague and surprise washed over their faces.

"You think I don't know? You think I don't know what goes on in my own house?"

Here, it seemed that the shock of learning the extent of Montague's information served to sober Cap up just a bit. He glanced at Billy and held up his good hand to indicate that from that moment on, he would do the talking and that Billy should remain silent.

"What passes in your house?" Cap asked. "Tell me what you know, Monty, or what you think you know."

"Know I that you labored on a matter most grave for Prince Hamlet. Know I that he did retain thy services for a *fanciful* claim."

"You are a fecking *solicitor*," Cap growled. "What do you know of matters litigious?"

"I know, Charles, that you do labor on a dream. 'Tis of the ether, this idea that you might press a claim against the King of Denmark."

Capulet smiled.

"Oh? And why is that?"

"Charles, enough of this madness! Take the money! I've brought a letter backed by the Queen's own signature for your share. Bacon has doubled his offer, at my urging, Charles. I want nothing more than to see you made whole, put to comfort."

"Put to pasture?"

"Put *at ease*," Montague said. "This...*claim*...if that be a fair name for it, will destroy what little fortune you must have left. You will be outnumbered, Charles. Out spent."

"I have the high ground," Cap said.

"You will be buried, Charles. The King's men will assail you at every possible encounter. You think he will bow to you and to Hamlet? Do you think that he will settle? If your silly claim be true, then you do now deal against a man who deals in *death*—yet you think he will settle on terms?"

"I know not," Cap said. "But I know I have the high ground."

"And you'll push this, then, to culmination? Where, Charles, wilt thou litigate this matter? Not in England. Not in Denmark, where they would surely have your head. And if you found venue for your willful and wanton litigation, then what? He will employ the finest legal minds in the Kingdom. His men will open the gates of Hell and from it will spew forth challenges to jurisdiction and motions in limine. His motions to suppress will be more numerous than the grains of sand on Devonshire's beaches. His men will tie thee up with motions to dismiss, with allegations that you fail to state a claim, with a thousand years of jurisprudence supportive of the notion that *your man hath no claim upon which action doth lie*. At each stage, you will see your fortunes diminishing. Will you mortgage your house for this devilish pursuit? You will lose it. Will you sell your family's estate in Wales? You will lose that, too. Your wife? She'll leave you, Charles. And if, if, IF, you manage to push this travesty to trial, then he will send forth discovery documents so numerous that they will blot out the Sun. What then, Charles?"

Charles stood, used his good hand to put his bad hand into the pocket of his housecoat, then leaned forward across the table. His face took on the look of a demon or a man possessed.

"Then we will litigate in the shade."

Cut to: Black.

EPISODE 8:

The Course of True Love

THE OFFICES OF C.APULET & MONTAGUE BUZZED. The offense of Montague's offer set Capulet on a legal tear the likes of which had not been seen in Birmingham since a young and idealistic Pict attorney had attempted to press charges of genocide against the Saxon invaders (and was summarily beheaded in the town square). Capulet was like a new man: a man possessed, an ambitious and energetic man, though crippled. Driven by this newfound zeal, he secretly mortgaged his home *and* his estates in Wales to fund the Hamlet matter. He exploded into the C.Ap.Ulet & Montague offices waving a three-page document and shouting for Montague. Behind him were Billy Shakespeare and Horatio the Git.

"What is the meaning of this?" Montague cried.

"Read it and weap at what thou hast just read!" Cap shouted. He slapped the documents against Montague's chest and then walked limply around the office, staring down anyone who dared to look at him as Montague read. Cap smiled ear-to-ear.

"An injunction?" Montague groaned.

"Old Paunchy Jones!" Cap said. "Seems Magistrate Jones is quite in agreeance with me on this point: Thou canst not rid me of these halls with such ease, Monty. Adwen!"

Adwen peaked her head into the main waiting room from the hallway.

"Sir?"

"See to it that the scoundrels do hoist high the C.Ap.Ulet sign, and fly the flag of Wales, M'Girl!"

"Yes, Sir!" Adwen answered gaily.[9]

"But this is madness," Montague argued. "And how is it that Magistrate Jones would even entertain the idea of helping you? Last I knew the man hated you."

"Set things right!" Cap interrupted him. "I set my mind to consideration of bygone days and came to certain realizations that had hitherto escaped my coarse nature. Turns out that, upon reflection, perhaps Selwyn Llewellen was *well within her rights as a woman* to choose her own life mate. She chose Paunchy and I've come to terms with that."

"When it suited you to come to terms with it!"

"Better late than never. Marched over to Paunchy Jones and apologized. I even extended to them an olive branch in the form of a savory steak and kidney pudding. It was a *pudding of peace*, if you will. Now, swathed as we are in the warm embrace of *pax boudin*, we are one big happy family again, as cousins should be. Selwyn and I are growing quite close. Monty, we'll be using my wing of the firm for the foreseeable future. Of course, *if you'd like*, you might march

---

[9] **Editor's Note**: Again, integrity requires that we point out that Adwen did not actually get around to having the C.Ap.Ulet name added back to the sign outside, although she did manage to have one of her friends remove the name "Bacon".

your poncy ass down to the magistrate's office and go a round or two with me over this injunction? No? No, I thought not."

Cap rounded up his men—Billy and Horatio—and together they disappeared into the dark side of the building where Cap's empty offices were about to bounce back to life after a brief, three-day emptiness. He saw Horatio back to his old office, then took Billy into his own office and shut the door behind him.

"We've only a few weeks, Billy."

"Yes?"

"Yes. Monty wouldn't dare address a magistrate for redress of grievances, as he is but a lowly solicitor. But he'll send word to Bacon and Bacon will have my injunction overturned in an hour. Our injunction from Jones will stand for now, but Paunchy Jones rates about a 3 on the "Magistrate Influence Index". So, we are working against a deadline, Shakes."

Montague and his team were, as always, busy preparing documents on seisin rituals and on grants of lands and lordships for the Birmingham gentry. It was primarily a contractual or "business-side" practice with Montague, for Montague had always feared the courtroom. But Capulet's small team was busy preparing for *trial*, for a *real trial*. Most importantly, they spent days and days producing large graphs detailing the vast real estate holdings of the Danish Crown.

Slowly, Horatio took on more responsibility, and that put fear in Capulet's heart because, although Horatio was well-trained at a respected school, he was a bit of a fool. Often, the three of them stayed at the office and worked all through the night. Documents and drafts of documents began to pile up in their offices as they put their minds around the coming case. They met in secret.

"Soft you, now, Montague comes," Capulet said. They huddled low around Capulet's desk and waited. Three raps upon the door, but they did not answer. They waited until Montague's footsteps marched away down the corridor.

"The coast is clear. Montague is gone. He must not know of this case in detail, understood? Good. Hand me that parchment, Will, and steady your quill, Horatio, we'll need notes. Are you up to the task?"

"Of note-taking? Yes, Sir. I read the law at Oxford, after all."

"Ponce College," Capulet snorted. "Horatio, be judicious in thy note taking. First, we must determine our *strategy*. That is, do we intend to prosecute this claim to sweet culmination, or do we ride for Elsinore and settlement? How say you, Will?"

"Justice, Sir. We seek justice for the aggrieved. Therefore, we do ready for trial."

"As you say. First—if this dread case does go to trial, 'twill be an endeavor most expensive."

"How expensive, Sir? I've no idea what a trial costs."

"Quite expensive. Our first matter must be to estimate what we will need in financing. Horatio, to your notes. We'll need paper and pencils, of course, both in great abundance, as well as quill and ink. Research costs shall not be modest. And we shall need room and board for our team abroad."

"Abroad, Sir?" Horatio asked.

"Yes, abroad!" Capulet shouted. He shook his head. "Horatio, how is it that you would think we could prosecute this action from *here* where our courts are wont of jurisdiction over the Danish King? Of course abroad!"

"So, Denmark?"

"Yes, yes, of course Denmark, Horatio. *If we'd like to be drawn and quartered after arguing in front of the King's own bench.* No, I think that won't do at all. Horatio, I think what you could do to really help on this case, in this first instance, is to estimate how much it will cost this office to prosecute this action. Estimate on 5 of us abroad, in The Hague, for six months."

"Six months?!" Billy asked.

"Belgium?" Horatio asked.

"Trials are long affairs, Will. And the King will delay and delay and delay. Horatio, are you up to it?"

"Yes, Sir."

"Good. Do an estimate for Copenhagen, as well, worst case scenario. But better focus on The Hague."

"In Belgium?" Horatio asked again.

"Belgium? By Jove, Horatio—are you a Catholic? I had no idea. *El Horatio Fernandes.* Eh, takes all kinds. No, The Hague is where it has always been, in Holland, in The Republic of the Seven United Netherlands. Belgium? How could The Hague be in Belgium?"[10]

---

[10] **Editor's Note:** None of our interns had *any* idea what Capulet was talking about here. But after some research we discovered that, when *SHAKESPEARE! Unwritten!* was filmed, the Low Countries of Belgium, the Netherlands, and Luxembourg were actually split roughly into two: the Southern Netherlands, or "Catholic Netherlands", which included present-day Belgium, and the Northern Netherlands, or the "Republic of the Seven United Netherlands", which included both The Hague and present-day Holland. The Southern Netherlands were ruled more-or-less by Spain and were aligned with Catholic interests.

Capulet smiled broadly. It was like life was breathing back into his dour face.

"Anyway, yes. 'Tis possible that we might negotiate a change of venue. Hamlet is likely to request a change of venue out of Copenhagen for fear that Claudius does hold sway over the local magistrates. Now, Will, to you—raise thy spirits and upon my charge begin preparation of discovery requests. 'Twill be a document production most grand. In league, you and I will draft the request in language most broad."

"Yes, Sir," Billy responded.

"We'll want record of all the comings and goings at Castle Elsinore. Appointment calendar for Hamlet and for the King, of course—"

"The late king or Claudius?" Horatio asked.

"Both! We'll want the castle receipts as well if, by some chance, Claudius did make purchase of a murder weapon. Are you getting all of this, Horatio?"

"Yes, Sir, Cap. Now should we also begin with the deposition schedule, Sir, and the table of evidentiary issues?"

"Not yet—before we know what evidence we will develop, we must determine what evidence we *must* develop. Circle in, Boys, and let me explain something to you. A trial must not be a thing so tedious. The jury will not find the truth on a ledger ready-made, but will divine their verdict from the story that we weave, a story delightful and of excellent fancy. This trial is not about evidence. *For we have none!* 'Tis not about depositions and motions in limine. 'Tis about the *story*, Horatio. Will—what is our *theory* of the case? I will play the jury."

"Yes, Sir. A case of greed and envy, Sir. Hamlet's uncle, Claudius, was jealous of his own brother's success. Claudius wanted the throne, thought he *deserved* it and that he could do the job better than Hamlet's father, the King."

"So we are to believe that simple greed drove Claudius to an act so vile?"

"Not greed alone, Sir. But envy and lust, to boot. We will show that Claudius and the Queen Gertrude were lovers."

"Lovers?" Capulet asked, his eyes wide as if taking on the role of a shocked juror. "What proof have we?"

"Proof, Sir? Need we proof of their lascivious trysting prior to the murder? No. Those dread lovers were bound in matrimony before the murdered King cooled in his grave."

"Yes! Money and the woman's wiles. That's motive. Opportunity?"

"Sir, opportunity did abound. We shall show that Claudius did set upon his brother, the King, *in* Castle Elsinore as his own brother lay sleeping."

"Murder weapon?" Capulet asked.

"Ay. There's the rub, Sir."

"No murder weapon? You expect me to convict without a murder weapon? You ask we, this Noble Jury, to convict and find damages although you cannot describe to me the vile machination by which Claudius exacted his murderous toll?"

"Yes, well, we're working on that."

"I've an idea, Sir," Horatio said. He put his quill down and took on the aspect of a thinking man.

"Speak," Capulet commanded.

"Perhaps Claudius approached and did poison the King."

"Poison? Poison? By what means? The King was sleeping, so our own witness will testify. Is poison not a dish best served cold with supper?" Capulet took great delight in his portrayal of the jury.

"Yes, Sir. Well, maybe he delivered it through other means, Sir."

"Other means? By what sorcery? I suppose he could inject it direct into the blood?" He and Billy laughed but Horatio was not discouraged.

"No, Sir," Horatio said. He spoke now forcefully. "I mean to say: The King was sleeping, correct? And do Kings not sleep just as the rest of us, not erect as a man walking, but reclining on one's side?"

"Go on?" Capulet said.

"His...ear...was exposed, Sir. Perhaps Claudius did pour a potion most noxious into the King's ear."

Neither Billy nor Capulet spoke, nor did they laugh. They furrowed their brows and moments passed in silence.

Then Capulet said, "Yes, well. Let's circle back up on that tomorrow. Boddy, if this be our theory of the case, then what be our proof?"

"We do lack on that score, Sir. We've only the testimony of the King himself."

"As I understand it, Sir," Horatio broke in, "the late King did identify his murderer. I'm at a loss as to what further proof be required."

"'Tis a question of *admissibility*, Horatio. Of course the King's testimony is all the proof we would need, however, and I would think you would know this, having read law at Ponce College, *spectral testimony is generally considered hearsay and is not admissible to prove guilt."*

"But the King told Hamlet who killed him?!" Horatio said.

"Do you not hear, Horatio—'tis *inadmissible* as proof. Do you not understand? 'Tis the rule that spectral testimony is inadmissible when offered to prove the truth of the matter asserted by the horrible spectre.[11] Did they not teach you this in Ponce College?"

"No, they did, Sir. My apologies. Evidence was my worst grade. But it seems to me that the *key* to the case is the King's testimony."

"Yes, Horatio, we *all* agree as to that point. What we do not yet agree on is how it might be possible to overcome the well-settled exclusion on spectral testimony. 'Twould seem that you have no ideas on that point, either." Having grown tired of Horatio he turned to Will. "Successful consummation on this action might there depend, Will. Ponce Horatio, though apparently an idiot, does respect the power of the King's testimony."

"I agree, Sir. And I have an idea—although 'tis a longshot," Billy said. "I happen to know the leading expert on matters evidentiary in the Kingdom. He does work in our very office. Though he does currently labor for Lord Montague."

"Of whom do you speak, Will?"

"Of Flavius, Sir."

---

[11] **Editor's Note:** This general rule of evidence still applies, though today we refer to this as the rule against *hearsay* evidence. The rule against hearsay evidence is quite complicated, but the short version of the rule is this: If something was said *out of court*, by someone who is *not in court*, then those statements cannot be offered to *prove the truth of the matter asserted* in those statements. The rule is subject to quite a few exceptions.

"Flavius?"

"Yes, Sir. He did extensive work on matters evidentiary while reading the law. I believe he wrote an article for the Oxford review. He worked very closely with Smith."

"Smith who wrote the Treatise on Evidence?"

"Yes," Billy said.

"But can you achieve him for our team? And can you do so without letting Montague know of our potentially lucrative action?"

"That I do not know, Sir. But I intend to try."

"So, then let us review," Capulet said. "The trial will be very expensive, our theory of the murder involves pouring noxious poison into the king's ear, and the only proof we have for this proposition is the spectral testimony of the dead king himself? Is that an accurate review of our current state?

"That's about the size of it, Sir."

Capulet thought for a moment, then spoke:

"Will—have the ponies fed. Tonight we ride for Castle Elsinore."

ACT III

EPISODE 9:

The Soul of Wit

BILLY AND CAPULET RODE FOR CASTLE ELSINORE in July of 1585 after weeks of hemming and some hawing. Billy wrote to his wife, now in her new city of London,[12] and his voice read those words over images of his travels with Capulet.

"My Dearest Anne.

These simple words of mine to you: Good Health,

And may these words quicken to you, my Heart.

I write to thee from the darkest of Denmark,

Where arrived my Lord and I well, though drunk.

We were two days London-bound for transfer

Cross the Channel unto darkest Denmark

When good souls along the road informed us,

---

[12] **Editor's Note:** At this point in this series, the director begins using montages and voiceovers. Some of the montages are still shots, pictures presumably taken by one of the crew, and some of the montages are simply clips of Shakespeare going about his business. *SHAKESEPEARE! Unwritten!* is highly derivative of Ken Burns's work. On top of these montages the director puts old English folk tunes played on the guitar and a voiceover artist reads Shakespeare's words. The voiceover artist is *not* Shakespeare. The voice chosen for the voiceover sounds very much like you *would think* Shakespeare would sound. In reality, Shakespeare's voice was a bit whiny, a bit tinny, and on the whole rather unimpressive.

That Denmark lay not across the Channel
As I had previously surmis'ed
But across the Northern Sea most hostile.
We were then four days more bound north for Hull,
For passage upon the seventh fastest
Clipper ship in Her Majesty's navy.
We found no ally in Neptune's high seas,
Tossed about as apples in the bushel.
Yet we now arrive at Kronborg swiftly,
Where sits Castle Elsinore and the King.
Bid us fierce luck unto the King's chambers,
And write me back if to do so be just.
As Always, Yours, Billy."

Billy and Capulet checked in with the concierge at Castle Elsinore on a very hot day in Denmark. The Castle was dark, imposing even, shrouded beneath a pallor of rain clouds that lowered over the Castle. The rest of Denmark was sunny.

Castle Elsinore was a busy place that hummed with activity and that had the look of an office park. At one end of the officious castle, beyond a corridor that separated the comings and goings of those employed at the castle from the quiet of the castle's on-site hotel, stood a wooden concierge desk. The concierge was a bulbous fellow, bald, and who looked to be on the verge of having a heart attack. There were chickens roaming around the castle freely, often nesting in piles of straw.

"One room?" the concierge asked and flipped through a book of bound parchment.

"No," Capulet said. He shook his head. "I wrote ahead for two rooms."

"Oh," the concierge said. "My mistake I thought you said one room." He giggled at Capulet and Shakespeare.

"Two," Capulet said again.

The concierge ran his finger down the long parchment ledger.

"Smoking or non-smoking?"

"What's the difference?" Billy asked.

"The non-smoking rooms have straw beds."

"And the smoking rooms?" Billy asked.

"No beds. Don't want the castle burning down, do we?"

"We'll take non-smoking," Capulet said.

"Why would it matter?" Billy asked. "I mean, the whole castle is stone, correct?"

"Yes, 'tis a stone castle," the concierge answered. "It's the finest of modern Danish design. Castle Elsinore is a sleek and inviting castle, built with luxury and security in mind. We are powered entirely by locally sourced hardwoods and clean Swansea coal, and we are very proud of our LAAD certification." He slid the registration forms across the table and Capulet and Billy scanned them and signed them.

"LAAD certification?" Cap asked.

"Yes, that's Leadership in Avoiding Asphyxiation Deaths. Our team of Scandinavian architects and designers utilized a holistic approach to incorporate ventilation into the overall aesthetic of the castle. So it is very, very rare for a person to asphyxiate when staying in any of our rooms."

"You hear that?" Cap said to Hamlet. "Safety first."

"Yes, could you just sign there, Sir? Yes, there. And there, for the waiver of liability."

"I'm not reading this," Cap said. "I'm just signing wherever you point."

Billy had not been paying attention, as he was still confused by the non-smoking policy.

"But if it is a *stone* castle, then could it even burn?"

"I don't *make* the rules," the concierge answered.

"I'm sure you don't. It's just that it doesn't make sense to me. I can't imagine a castle burning down."

"They do sometimes," Capulet said. "I've heard that they do from time to time. No matter. Let's get to our rooms and sober up. We've an important meeting tomorrow."

A bellboy wearing tattered clothes and dung-soiled shoes helped them carry their bags to their rooms. They each slept like dogs that night in piles of straw in a dark room with sweating walls of smoke stained stone.

The next day they splashed themselves in cold water then went to the public bath for a very thorough cleaning. They were very thoroughly cleaned. After their bath they put on their finest suits, each with very puffy shoulders and large frilled collars. They looked tight. They headed back to the Castle and walked briskly down damp stone hallways toward the King's chambers.

"Carry a folio," Capulet said.

"What's that?"

"Go back to your room and get a folio. 'Tis important to have a folio when you enter a negotiation. They'll wonder what's in it."

"Right."

Billly returned to his room and then returned with his folio and they walked together the length of Castle Elsinore. They reached the king's antechamber and checked in with King Claudius's secretary.

"He's awfully busy," she said. "This is going to be quite a day around here. He's pushed you two from 9:30 to 10:15 already."

"Quarter past ten?" Capulet asked, then sighed. "Well, we'll wait. Looks like we'll be here another night."

"Would you like me to send word down to the concierge?" the secretary asked.

"You better do, Sweetie," Capulet said. "We'll just sit over here, I suppose."

They sat in the waiting room until 10:15 and then the secretary said that Claudius had pushed their meeting to 11:05. So they waited until 11:05 and were then told that it was pushed until 1:10 after lunch. So they went out for lunch and returned to find that they'd been pushed to 2:40.

"Claudius apologizes," his secretary said. "He wants you to know that he will not push your meeting again. It is 2:40, in stone."

"Capital," Capulet said.

He and Billy sat down again and waited. They began to get nervous as they closed in on their 2:40 meeting.

"Stop fidgeting," Capulet said to Billy.

"I'm not fidgeting, Sir."

"No, you're fidgeting. I can feel mine own chair shaking from your fidgeting."

"Respectfully, Sir, I am not fidgeting. In fact, if I may be so bold, 'tis you that are fidgeting."

Capulet looked down and saw that it was indeed his own leg twitching.

"Why yes. It would appear that I am fidgeting. Well. Order me to stop fidgeting, Willy. Does me no good to be nervous."

"I don't have that authority."

"I am to you delegating such authority, Will."

"Stop fidgeting, Sir."

"Thank you, Will. Remember, be deferential in there. We must be deferential. Hast thou met previously with a King?"

"I have not, Sir."

"Be deferential. Remember that a king is just like you and me, but better. They respond only to deference. And don't look him in the eye."

"Like a bear, Sir?"

"Yes, much like a bear. No sudden movements. Try not to scare him. Try to appear…larger. And remember, he's just as scared of you as you are of him."

"Really?"

"No, not in the least. But remember it, anyway."

The secretary rose from behind her desk and walked out into the waiting room with a paper in her had.

"Ap Ulet and Shakespeare? The King will see you now. You'll have five minutes, no more. He is very busy today."

"Thank you," Capulet said.

She led them both into the King's royal office. It was large, almost cavernous, and their footsteps sent regal echoes bouncing off the moist stone walls. Claudius himself stood in a long purple robe beside a roaring fire, though it was in fact very warm that day. He had his crown on, which was his manner in those days.

"Your Royal Highness. 'Tis our greatest honor that you have been so cordial as to entertain our entreaty unto thee," Capulet said. He and Billy both performed a grand bow—or, at least, Capulet bowed as grandly as he could, his disabilities notwithstanding. Claudius turned to them.

"Go on. What business hast thee?" He almost sang when he spoke. Claudius was a strange and evil man.

"Good King, Your Highness, we come in the stead and in representation of the young Prince Hamlet."

"Hamlet? What's he want, now? An increase in his royal allowance, no doubt. How much does he beg me this week?"

"With respect, Good King, Your Highness, we are not here with regard to the Prince's allowance. Rather, we do represent the young Hamlet on a matter of more grave significance."

"Out with it. I've not got all day."

"Good King, Your Highness, the young Hamlet does intend to prosecute against you and we have come offering terms in this respect."

"Terms?"

"Yes, Good King, Your Highness. We are empowered by our client to offer to you terms of settlement in this matter."

"He offers terms? To me? And what action, pray thee, would Hamlet prosecute against me?"

"Good King, Your Highness, wrongful death."

"Wrongful death? What manner of a trespass is *wrongful death*? I say that is poppy cock."

"Good King, Your Highness, the Prince does intend to prosecute trespass *on the case*[13] of wrongful death in the demise of his late father, your brother."

The King laughed and his grand belly shook.

"Wrongful death? Ap Ulet—was that your name?"

"'Tis *Lord* Ap Ulet, Your Highness, Good King, though 'tis rendered *Capulet* in English."

"Yes, well, *Lord* Capulet. Hamlet seeks settlement from *me?* I have heard the argument, and there is great offense in it. And can you by no drift of circumstance get from *him* why he puts on this confusion, grating so harshly all his days of quiet with turbulent and dangerous lunacy?"

"Good King, Your Highness—"

"Have thee any idea how many actions are against this office prosecuted daily, Capulet?"

"I do not, Good King. Your Highness."

---

[13] **Editor's Note:** Oh, blah! Law stuff is so boring! Thankfully, the filmmakers didn't even bother *trying* to explain the difference between "trespass" and "trespass on the case". As the editor, I feel like I'm bound to explain the difference to non-lawyer readers. But I don't want to. Sigh. Here we go: Look at it this way, if a man named John punches a man named Frank, then Frank would have a trespass action against John. If, instead, John punched a donkey and then the donkey kicked Frank, then Frank might *not* have a trespass action against John because John didn't actually touch Frank, but he might have an action of trespass on the case. Basically, all the long-standing and traditional torts—like battery—were styled as trespass actions, but new tort theories that hadn't yet been tested in court—like "wrongful death" for our purposes—were styled as trespass on the case. It's really just old-tymy legal mumbo-jumbo that we'd all be better off to just forget about.

"And, pray, have thee then any idea how many attorneys we do employ upon retainer for this office, this crown?"

"I confess it, Good King, that I do not know. Your Highness."

"And have thee any notion *whatsoever* of the gravity of matters business that this office does entertain on the daily? No?"

"I confess, Sir, Good King, Your Highness, that I have not such a notion."

"I suppose that you would not. *You* must not think that I am made of stuff so flat and dull that I can let my beard be shook with danger, and think it pastime. And yet, young Hamlet, himself from royal teat yet to be weaned, expects me to be intimidated into settlement by limping, and limp, sheep shagging Welshmen with fanciful claims of *wrongful* death? For damages, no doubt? I should expect as much from my nephew, but 'tis a grave indictment on the state of those men called before the bar of Wales that you would entertain such foolishness. Now, have thee more to say on the matter or will that suffice for consideration?"

"Uh—" Capulet began, but Claudius interrupted him.

"No, I thought not. If thou hast more to say, take it up with my attorney on this matter, Sir Francis Bacon of London. You are dismissed."

Billy took Capulet by the arm to restrain him, but could not; Capulet spoke:

"I do wish a word more, Your Highness. King. We may be Welsh, so born by cruelest Fate, that same Fate who my form dissembled. But upon my honor, I swear it, Good King, to God and to our St. David: that the same cruel Fate my misfortunes made shall yield up unto me thy wicked crown. I bid thee good day."

Capulet and Billy turned to exit the office.

"You are a funny little man," Claudius said as they left.

"GOOD DAY!" Capulet shouted behind him.

Capulet and Billy marched directly to their rooms where they gathered their bags and checked out of Castle Elsinore. "I'd rather sleep on the docks than in this castle!" Capulet complained. They walked to the docks and, as it was quite warm out, decided to sleep there. They found a nice quiet place to sit and lay out their cloaks for beds and there they lay down beside the writhing sea and the boats that came and went throughout the night.

"Well that didn't go quite as well as expected," Billy said.

"Didn't go well? Why, we have him by the short hairs. Did you not see him trembling? He was most certainly in a condition of fright when we took leave. I should say he'll cave before we reach trial."

"Do you think so?" Billy asked.

"I do! I must, indeed, for it pains the just man to think the world unjust, and the good man to think the world wicked. No, do not have fear in your heart, Will—we shall have him."

"Really, Sir?"

"Likely," Capulet answered. He rolled over to go to sleep.

"Really, Sir?"

Capulet sighed.

"Much of *me* depends upon this action. Please joke no more, protect my gentle self."

Slowly at first, and then with haste and indiscretion, the Sun set over Castle Elsinore and the two attorneys sleeping on the street beside the harbor. Capulet was fast to sleep but Billy could not bring himself to relax. He pulled his journal from his folio and wrote:

"My Dearest Anne, We are forsaken. Please write back to me. As Always, Yours, Billy."

EPISODE 10:

The Game is Afoot

BILLY AND CAPULET RETURNED TO BIRMINGHAM after failing to negotiate a settlement with Claudius, the King of Denmark. Their client, Prince Hamlet of Denmark, was quite well known among the European literati as a man who traveled constantly, always gathering research and material for his "novel". The Prince's peripatetic schedule, coupled with the horrid state of communication in 16th Century Europe, made communication between Capulet and his client difficult. They received a letter by courier from Hamlet when they had not yet returned to Birmingham. They were several miles outside of Birmingham when a courier approached.

"Lord Capulet?" the Courier asked.

"'Tis I," Capulet answered from atop his pony. The courier turned his pony around and rode along side them.

"Tim Gildenstern, Sir, with the King's Courier service. Post for you, Sir," the courier said as he handed the letter to Capulet.

"'Tis the seal of Prince Hamlet," Capulet said to Billy, and he ripped open the letter. He spoke as he read. "Yes. Yes. Yes. Capital. Capital. Thank you, Gildenstern."

"And shall I carry back a message?" Gildenstern asked.

"No," Capulet answered. "No reply is requested. Shall we need your services, we shall enquire with the King's Courier office."

"Very well," the courier said and was off at a trot.

"You see that!" Capulet said. "You see that! That's *service*, Willy. Service."

"The King's Courier is really turning itself around these days. Must be laying the smack down in London, Sir."

"I should say so. Imagine if we had a courier service like the French do. We'd be a top-rate nation in no time."

"Well, that and the schools, Sir."

"Of course. Yes, of course we need better schools. But one thing at a time, Willy. At any rate—the good Prince begs we press on in our action. He received word from Bacon's office that his uncle would not settle."

"Our next move, Sir?" Billy asked.

"'Tis completed already," Capulet answered. "Took care of it while we were in Kronborg."

"Yes?"

"Retained local counsel in The Hague through the Copenhagen office of a little Dutch firm. With any luck they've filed the action already at The Hague, with request made to King Claudius that he accept jurisdiction. I believe he'll accept—did you not hear him let it slip that he's retained Bacon?"

"I did, Sir," Billy answered.

"Bacon is…he's a smart man, Willy. He's the leading jurist in the Kingdom. Do you follow me?"

"I do, I think," Billy answered.

"Francis Bacon is perhaps the smartest man in all of England; he is a fine advocate and he is the finest jurist. I clerked with his offices in London after reading the law. But he is a ponce."

"Is he?"

"Of the highest order," Capulet answered. "You met him! He fancies himself a barber of the human condition and holds in highest regard his own counsel regarding matters of the public opinion. I have little doubt but that he shall advise Claudius to accept jurisdiction in The Hague, rather than to have this sordid matter played out on the stage of the Danish broadsheets. And yet Bacon did come to Birmingham seeking to buy my law offices? Do you not think that telling?"

They rode several yards in relative silence.

"So it has begun, then?" Billy asked.

"Yes. The game is afoot."

"I expected it to feel different than this," Billy said. "It is my first trial, Sir. As you know. And I thought...I'm not sure what I thought. But I thought it would feel somewhat different."

"Didst thou expect wine and song?"

"Good faith, Sir, yes. I thought there would be a bit more pomp."

"Would that there were a moment of celebration," Capulet agreed. "We shall not celebrate yet again many weeks, I'm afraid. Nay...months."

"Sir?"

"Speak, Willy."

"Will we win this case?"

"I know not," Capulet admitted. His face grew stern and Billy thought that Capulet might be slipping again into one of his dour, depressed moods. "Shall I speak in truth with thee, my Second Chair?"

"Do," Billy answered. "I beg thee, do. "

"We've not much of a case, Willy. We have no evidence at all to place Claudius in the King's chambers that dreadful night, nor have we even a believable...*hypothesis* as to how Claudius accomplished the dread task. We have no murder weapon. We have only the testimony of the late King, and, speaking frankly with thee, I do not think it admissible."

"Flavius will find the way for us," Billy said. "If such testimony *can* be admitted, he will find the way."

"I admire the folly and force of thy youth," Capulet said. "But do be steady with me this moment. It has never happened that a matter so grave be decided by spectral testimony. Claudius must know our case—he has been preparing. He must have, for he did retain Bacon, who has been the leading voice in English jurisprudence lo these many years regarding exclusionary evidentiary principles. Bacon has written *extensively* on how unreliable spectral testimony is. Shall we speak of principles? If we do speak of principles, then I admit that I agree with Sir Bacon. Spectral testimony is—well, it's less than reliable."

"On account of people not remembering it accurately? Or on account of lying specters?"

"Poor memory, of course! Spectres are unable to lie, I believe. That's how I've always understood it. But know this, Will: We have the high ground. And know I now that Bacon's untimely arrival in our own halls was not untimely in truth, but a scheme most devious."

"Sir?"

"Think you that it was a coincidence that Bacon appeared, offering me a King's Ransom for my share of our petty little Birmingham shit hole? Think you that Sir Francis Bacon woke one morning thinking, 'I'd like to have a nice little solicitor's office in Birmingham!' No, I think not."

"Do I hear thee correctly? That you now charge that Sir Francis Bacon set his sights on *your* practice on account of this Hamlet matter?"

"He is a man as devious as he is sharp."

"Sir? If you've a moment, tell me truly, why are thou so despised of Bacon?"

"He is a phenomenal man, truly," Capulet admitted. "In truth, I agree with his approach to the laws of evidence as well as to the role of *reason* in the law. I have tremendous respect for him as a thinker, Willy. But I hate the man, too, for he did not hire me after my apprenticeship with his office on account of my Welshness."

"But he had to have known when he took you on as apprentice?"

"No. I was passing," Capulet answered. He looked ashamed.

"You!?" Billy laughed. "You? Passing as Anglo?"

"It was a strange time," Capulet said. "Less said about it, the better. Now, I to Birmingham and you to Stratford-upon-Avon. Take two days, or three if you need, to recuperate from this trip. Then, back to the office."

"And you, Sir? Time off?"

"Ha. No rest for the wicked when the game is afoot, Willy Boy. I'm away to the office this evening. See you in three days."

Episode 11:

Cry Havoc!

WEEKS PASSED as Billy, Capulet, and Horatio worked on the upcoming trial. They set October 1st as the day they would leave for The Hague, and officials at Castle Elsinore agreed to have the document discovery request met by or before October 7th by delivery to The Hague. In the meantime, Horatio made arrangements for their team, which had grown to include six clerks from the clerk pool, to travel and work in the The Hague. Capulet and Billy spent long days mocking up arguments and drafting pleadings. They spent even longer hours in futile attempts to research an answer to their evidentiary problem. Flavius was their only hope.

Almost two weeks to the day after returning from Denmark, Billy was working late when Flavius knocked on his door.

"Billy?" he asked, and opened the door enough to peer in. "Still working?"

"Yes!" Billy answered. "Do come in."

"About to head back for Stratford, Bill. Are you joining me this evening, or cutting out again like a ponce?"

"Staying here again tonight, I'm afraid," Billy answered. He leaned back in his chair and tossed his quill onto his desk. Flavius sat down in the guest chair opposite the desk.

"Come on!" Flavius whined. "Be thou serious? Yet again tonight?"

"I am serious."

"'Tis an awful commute without your company," Flavius said.

"'Tis an awful commute with or without my company," Billy corrected him. "'Tis on account of that commute in the main that Anne did grow to hate me."

"Yeah, sure," Flavius said. "On *that* account."

"A fig for thee," Billy said.

"How is thine Anne?" he asked Billly. Then, as Billy was not paying attention, he began in secret to pack up Billy's satchel for travel.

"She's not mine, I'd say," Billy said. "She's yet to write to me from London. I'm afraid the marriage is over."

"Over?" Flavius asked. "Well, I—"

"She grew angry every evening because I was so late in returning from Birmingham. Every evening, Flavius. I could do nothing with her. I swear, but to know your secret—how is it that your wife excuses such late return and you keep such a happy marriage?"

"She excuses me? Ha! She relishes my late return. No, we are not happy, Will. 'Tis quite a confusion of the mind and heart to wish a happy marriage. Better just to eat and drink and be merry."

"What are you doing? Packing my saddlebags?"

"Yes, you are joining me this evening on commute. I've decided. And I've a fine bottle of the *porto* for the ride home."

"Yes, yes. I suppose I should," Billy agreed. "But tell me again, she is not depressed of the hours that you keep?"

"At first she was, yes," Flavius agreed. "But, as she's grown to hate me over the years, she now thinks it nice that she has the run of the place for most of the day. She even keeps her own bed now. No, we are not in a 'happy' marriage. But 'tis for the best! 'Tis on this account that I've advanced so quickly at the firm. O! But the wives do hunger after the good man's time."

"I congratulate you, Flavius, your marriage. That you have not let it break beneath these pressures. Mine, I fear, has ended."

"Ended? What do you even mean?"

They left the offices and headed toward the stable.

"I mean 'to end', of course. Don't you ever worry about Loretta leaving you?"

"Leaving? Where would she go? Now that you mention it, might be quite nice if she left for a while. Wouldn't have to go sneaking about so much with the scullery wench."

"Well, perhaps our views differ on this matter," Billy said. He'd hoped to end the conversation.

"But sure they do!" Flavius said. He laughed and laughed. "I declare it, Will, that you are dear to my heart. But you are a confounding liberal soul. Why are you so depressed all the time? Because Anne left you? Ha! If a woman leaveth thee, 'tis on account of evil demons that do inhabit within. Everyone knows this. So better they go, anyway! So it cannot be Anne's departure that troubles you."

"I think it is, mostly," Billy said.

"We don't think so."

They handed their claim tickets to the stable boy and the boy was quick to bring their ponies.

"We?"

"Of course, we," Flavius said. "You think no one talks at the office? We think it's because you spend all your time with that dreadful Lord Capulet."

"Think ye not that he is a good man?" Billy asked.

"Good man? Maybe. Who knows? I know he's dour as all hell. He's like a rainstorm, Will. On your wedding day. Do you know what I mean?"

"Sort of," Billy answered. "Though I can't put my finger on it."

"Well, we all talk of this."

"Who? I command thee, tell me who speaks thusly of me and of Capulet?"

"Who doesn't!? Every associate in the office dreaded working for Capulet before he was fired—which was no great fear, as he has no work to give. The partners abhor him so, as well. Lord Montague, of course. And Lord Frederick's team can't stand the man. Adrian's men, as well. All the partners talk! They say he was not always of this disposition and was, indeed, a fine litigator some years back. But now, my God!, 'tis no wonder his practice suffers so!"

"His practice suffers?" Billy asked. "How know ye this?"

"His woman, that Welsh scamp Adwen, she turned in his time sheets of a week before he was relieved his partnership. Or what little of time sheets he had to report. Indeed, why think you that Lord Montague conspired with Sir Francis Bacon to see Capulet relieved of his partnership? 'Twas either that or relieving him of profits on account of his dismal hours. Had you not heard of the naming news?

No, I suppose you hadn't. Lord Montague has not yet succeeded in evicting Capulet from the halls—though in short order he will see sweet culmination on such motion—but he has succeeded in attaining a declaration from Magistrate Johnson ordering the removal of Capulet's name from the signage, the letterhead. In very short order, the firm is to become The Law Offices of Montague & Frederick—and of course, I expect to see the addition of Bacon's name in the near season. Will raise my cache, won't it? Association with Bacon is a hell of a boon for a resume."

"But 'tis Lord Capulet who *founded* the firm!" Billy answered. He was growing angry now.

"Calm thyself!" Flavius said. Billy tried to swallow his emotions. "Yes, 'tis a shame to see a good man tumble. Montague tells me on my confidence, which I now relate to you upon fear of harsh recourse, that Capulet is on the way out. *In the head*, he says. And you best sleep with an eye open, too, Bill, as just this past week on the links, Lord Montague questioned the source of your devotion to the dour barrister."

"Do you not know?" Billy asked him. "But seriously, Man, do you not know?"

"No. We know not. Do tell me."

"We are kinsmen," Billy pronounced.

"Kinsmen? But he's Welsh? Unless...oh, Will?"

"Yes," Billy answered proudly. "For five years have I lived inside this secret. I pray thee tell no one."

"But 'tis the juiciest gossip I've heard this week! You don't even *look* Welsh. O! But the boys at the office would get a kick out of this."

"I tell ye this upon thy confidence," Billy went on. "Flavius, I tell ye this because thou art so dear to me. Swear it that you will speak of it to no man and, on my word, I will tell you a greater secret."

"Speak, Dear Brother, if I may still consider thee a brother, and I swear it."

"Capulet's hours did suffer so for the sake of matters yet unbillable," Billy said. He sighed heavily after he'd said it, as if the secret had been weighing heavily on him.

"Unbillable? What sort of hours are these? Golfing hours?"

"No. 'Tis for a private client, Flavius. A high profile client."

"High profile client? Ha. What manner of case does he labor upon?"

"Trespass upon the case of wrongful death," Billy answered.

"Wrongful death? Is there such a thing as *wrongful* death? Or *rightful* death, for that matter? Does action lie thereon for wrongful death?"

"We believe it will," Billy said.

"Who is this, thy mysterious client?"

"Hamlet, Prince of Denmark," Billy answered.

"Hamlet?!" Flavius shouted, surprised. Billy nearly fell off his pony, leaning over to quiet Flavius. "Still you are on about this Hamlet matter?"

"SHH! SHH!"

Flavius gathered himself and spoke quietly.

"Hamlet? The novelist? But how does he pay thee?"

"Upon contingency," Billy answered.

"I do not understand," Flavius said. "If I may speak truthfully, Will, I fear that I share in Montague's assessment that Lord Capulet has lost his faculty of reason. A client with no money, who cannot pay, for a case on which action might not lie, against a distant defendant. Will cost a fortune to prosecute! And who is the defendant? Judgment proof, no doubt."

"We do press action against the crown of Denmark," Billy said. Flavius's smile fell and he looked at Billy as they rode. Neither spoke for several moments.

"'Twas not five months ago that the Lord King Claudius of Denmark, then brother of the King, did set upon and slew his own brother, the Late King."

"But was not Hamlet himself the heir-apparent?" Flavius asked. "So would he not stand to gain from such regicide?"

"He was. And Claudius then did deny Hamlet his princely throne. He also took the Good Queen Gertrude into his bed, and to her was he wed by law not three weeks after the death of his brother."

"The Danes are a strange people," Flavius said. "OK. But say that you *do* press this action and assuming, *arguendo*, that some magistrate finds that action thereon doth lie, what remedy does fair Hamlet seek?"

"Damages monetary."

"My God, Willy. Damages monetary? For the loss of his crown and kingdom."

"And of his beloved father," Billy added. "I confess it, our case stands now upon matters evidentiary. We are understaffed, Flavius. We've only a few clerks and that buffoon, Horatio, to labor upon this matter. I am now, upon charge of Capulet himself, bidding thee to join our team. I know you to be the most learned man in all the Kingdom upon matters evidentiary."

"Except Sir Francis Bacon," Flavius corrected.

"Well, of course, except Bacon. You are the second most learned man in the Kingdom upon matters evidentiary."

"Yes, but…were I to do so, Montague would fry me. I've got a good thing with Montague. Hours are good, friendly workmates."

"But do you *love* it?" Billy asked him. "Flavius? No, I should say you do not. For who could love such a bland existence as that of a mere solicitor on matters of estates and seisin. You and I both were called before the *bar*, Flavius. Come with me, and we will advocate for a client in despair. We will argue not on matters clerical, but on the matter of justice—justice for a kingdom's crown stolen and for a bereaved son. Come with me, Dear Flavius, and I swear it, you will have unitary reign to research and to write on this matter of evidence. And, Capulet may let you even argue the point if it goes to appeal, which it might. Plus, we'd be working in The Hague."

"In Belgium?"

"No, it's in the Netherlands. Why does everyone think it's in Belgium?"

"I'm pretty sure that it's in Belgium," Flavius said. "It's in Brussels. I'm almost sure."

"No, it's not. It's a city in the Netherlands."

"God. Will, but I must admit that does sound good. No one knows mine heart like you—I do wish to strut about before the bar. No one reads the law just to be a clerk filing papers. But I have duties, Will! I've a mortgage and a wife and fourteen or fifteen children to feed. How shall I feed them all, Will, with mine honor and contentment?"

"No! Course not. We're on contingency."

"And what of that? I know not what that even means."

"It means that, if…when…we win, Hamlet will receive damages monetary. Our agreement is that our team takes 50% and splits that among us."

"Say again?"

"Damages monetary for the loss of the crown of Denmark," Billy said, speaking very slowly. "We take 50% of *that*, and split it among the 10 of us—Cap, me, you, Horatio, and six clerks. The case turns on this evidence matter. So if you come through for us, you'll get almost the same share that I do."

"Say again?"

"You'll get 10% of 50% of Denmark."

"I'm in."

Let Slip the Dogs of War

FLAVIUS ARRIVED EARLY THAT MORNING to Billy's place in Stratford-upon-Avon to help him load bags into the carriage. Capulet, along with the clerks and the case materials, were to arrive by nine that morning to join Billy and Flavius in their caravan for the south of England. By the time Flavius arrived at Billy's place, Billy was already tossing his bags into the carriage.

"Hi-ho!" he shouted. His own carriage pulled alongside and Flavius jumped up quickly to gather his own bags from the back of the carriage and toss them into the carriage that Billy had already packed. "Hell of a night!"

"You're late," Billy said.

"The wife had me up all night long," Flavius said. He smiled. "If you catch my meaning."

"Yes. Your meaning is not lost on me, Good Flavius. And, if I speak truly, your jest was not subtle."

"Still...long night. Right? Right?"

"Yes. Long night," Billy agreed. "I gather that I would be misguided were I to entertain the foolish idea that you perhaps labored the night away on matters litigious?"

"Yes. Very foolish, indeed. I was engaged in more sporting pursuits. If you catch my meaning."

"Yes. And, again, I should say that your humor falls somewhere south of subtle. Let us hope that you make a better litigator than you do a comedian."

Flavius smiled a great deal and fumbled through his satchel, taking the last possible minute to verify that his wife had packed his passport and toiletries for him.

"To Holland!" Billy shouted.

"To Belgium!" Flavius shouted. He tossed his last satchel over to the carriage, paid his own carriage man, and settled into the back of the open-faced trailer with Billy. "Or the Netherlands! Or wherever!" Then, after taking stock of the low quality of their carriage, he said: "But we ride in style with thy man, Capulet!"

"Don't tease," Billy said. "We are on a budget."

"From the looks of it, 'on a budget' might be a bit of a stretch," Flavius said. "Looks more like we are very near a budget, though not quite upon a budget." Flavius waited for howls of laughter, but Billy did not laugh. "I say, perhaps if we were standing a bit higher we might be able to spy the budget." He waited. "No? Nothing? Tough crowd. But here comes your man Capulet now!" He pointed down Birmingham Avenue at a very large trailer pulled by two large draft horses. Capulet sat high up beside the carriage man and he swayed back and forth with the movement of the carriage.

"To Holland!" Billy shouted as Capulet's carriage arrived.

"To victory!" Capulet shouted back. "Let's away ourselves, Boys. We're on a schedule."

"Where are the clerks and Horatio?" Flavius asked.

"In back, with the documents," Capulet answered. "We're on a budget. You two up here with me for the time being."

The caravan formed and they began the slow crawl southward toward London and the River Thames.

"Boys," Capulet began. "When we make the coast, I will book passage for both of thee on return vessels. Open fare."

"Sir?"

"You know, just in case," Capulet said. "You keep your tickets close by your heart, Boys. For if we run into trouble in the Low Countries, you might need to beat a hasty retreat back to the Kingdom."

"Thank you, Sir," Billy said.

"Yes, well, it means a lot to me that both of you come along. I would not see you done wrong by this trial. So I *will* make your passage back to the Kingdom. In the meantime, let us do what we can to relax on this voyage, for we will not have much work respite once we're ashore in that dark country of the Netherlands. We will work, we will toil. It will be desperate times. But we're all in."

"All in," Flavius agreed.

"To the Hague!" Capulet said.

"TO BELGIUM!" Flavius and Billy shouted together. "Or wherever!" Then they opened a large bottle of the *porto* and began drinking.

ACT IV

EPISODE 13:

Depose the Ghost

THE CARAVAN MADE ASTOUNDING TIME to southern England and they were just as quick across the Channel where, to their surprise, they found that Horatio had arranged passage for the team to Brussels, Belgium. Upon confirming that The Hague was not in Belgium, in fact, but in the Netherlands, Capulet arranged for transport to that more appropriate destination. By October 1st, the team had set up shop in a small block of offices that Horatio had secured by lease while the team was still in Birmingham. The offices that Horatio had leased sight-unseen actually *were* in The Hague, which defied all logic and reason. Capulet was quite impressed with the new workspace, which Horatio had managed to lease at a very low price, and because Horatio had succeeded so profoundly with the offices while failing so profoundly at securing travel from England to The Hague, Capulet was certain that Horatio was a moron. Horatio oversaw the clerks as they unpacked and set up their law library; within a week they were housed in a fully functioning British law office in The Hague. On the 10th of October, they took delivery of several thousand documents from Castle Elsinore.

"My God," Horatio groaned. They all stood in the sunlight outside the office as the train of wagons rode up, each filled with copies of official documents from the Castle. Huge Danish workmen unloaded box after box of documents, each heavier than the last. "This will take us ages to review."

"Be strong," Capulet advised. "Be strong."

"We don't even know what we're looking for in these documents!" Horatio said.

"Shut up," Billy scolded him. "Just shut up, Horatio. We'll all pitch in, we'll all review. If there is *anything* in there that could help our case, we'll find it."

"When arrives Hamlet?" Flavius asked.

"Week next," Capulet answered. "Have you prepared for his deposition?"

"We are doing so," Flavius answered. "We'll be ready for him. And Claudius?"

"Not 'till December, I'm afraid."

"No matter," Flavius answered. "His is a throwaway. We'll get nothing from him. Bacon will see to that."

Capulet's team took up residence in a cheap hotel across the street from their offices. Capulet, Billy, and Flavius each took single rooms, but Horatio and the clerks were forced to stay dorm style. Capulet explained this by saying that the hotel did not have enough single rooms, but very quickly the clerks investigated and found out that this was not the case. Capulet grew angry and blamed the hotel for lying to him, but no change was made and the clerks remained bunked together in a single room.

At night, in his room, Billy drank rum and wrote to his wife.

"My Dearest Anne,

We have arrived The Hague for the trial

though I know not what fortunes here will be.

For good or ill, my fate to Capulet

be bound, and on this case do both depend."

Sometimes Billy grew angry, even while writing. This night, he grew angry and exclaimed out loud: "My God, but I miss thee, Anne. If but through some sorcery you might hear me *now!*" And, by some sorcery, she *did* appear to him in the very room, though no one else could have seen her had they been there. He conjured her up in his mind—or, more accurately, she was conjured into being by the trickery of the camera.

"Will!" the spectral Anne said. "Tell me, are *you* well?"

"Ah, what ghost! The trickery of man's lonely mind, or 'tis thee I see? I will delight in this imagination….

"We find our quarter here cramped, staid and low, sleeping na'er one o'er top the other's bunk. But food and drink be to us plentiful, Capulet sees to that. He'd have us drunk. It keeps what little our morale remains. Though I know not how he finances it."

"And of Brussels?" she asked him. "Tell me of Brussels!"

"What? Why does everyone think we're in Belgium? We're in *The Hague*—it's in the Netherlands! At any rate, Hospitable The Hague be a mystery, for we, in closed quarters, are kept daily engag'ed in infernal reviewing thousands of documents from Elsinore. We search for needles in this our haystack. Between this, research, and deposition, I've not seen the aureate Sun's visage since summer's longer days have pastured on."

"Billy," she said in his mind. "Billy, though I despise myself the notion, I am proud of you." This caused Billy to smile as he wrote. When the smile faded, he started to cry softly.

"How can I tell thee what now consumes me: I miss you, Anne, and long for commission. 'Twas not until we were apart entire that I understood how apart we were when near, each to each, in earthly repose. I did not know myself, nor know of thee. Tell, do you believe we've but this one life, or perhaps would we be born again strong, with our mistake's knowledge gleaned intimate, insulated we of these mortal pains?"

"I am neither priest nor philosopher," the Thought of Anne said in his mind, and on the screen. "I know only what I see before me— this one life lay out before us."

"What a fuckery I have made of this: my one life certain passes now unloved. And but one question on my life to prove: 'Twas it greed that ruined me, or was it love?"[14] Billy often cried when he wrote to Anne, because he did not know if she would read his words or simply toss them away with the rubbish. "Please write back. Yours, Always, Billy."

Meanwhile, hundreds of miles away in London, Anne thought: "Of course I'll write back, Billy. I love your letters."

Billy began to review his latest letter, and perhaps to refine it, but Capulet knocked and then bound in through the door.

"Boddy Shakes! We begin again."

"Yes, Sir. Of course, Sir."

---

[14] **Editor's Note:** To clear up a question of *accent*, when Shakespeare spoke, the words "prove" and "love" rhymed.

Capulet was no simpleton. He could hear loss and loneliness in Billy's voice. Capulet sat on the straw bed and reached out his good arm to Billy's shoulder.

"I know the pain that cause thy spirit's flight. To England? Where resides your true soul's seat. Ay. But heed it, Will, that we to this foreign clime are, for a time, to wed. 'Tis only work can free us from *this* unnatural matrimony. 'Tis work will make your passport back to England, to your wife, to her bed. She waits, Will. I know it in my heart. Now! Do work. Do work! DO WORK!"

"Yes, My Lord!" Billy answered.

EPISODE 14:

A Visit From the King

BILLY WROTE:

"My Dearest Anne, I write love to thee, again from The Hague, though the day dispose me to lower station. I dwell now within Lord Capulet's purse, for he no longer makes us our wages but in food, in drink, and board most humble. No delight but work for our diversion! The Dane King, insolent, delays the day, no doubt in hopes with time our passions slip, and by financial woe we lose our moorings. Such is this slothful war. Such is justice. Yet at long wait the day we consecrate when Hamlet and the King in trial sit, their star-crossed course before the Law aligns. And in that course, my fate determin'ed. Yet I beg not before the Law's command, but to you, and Love's mortal sovereignty—Bid me back at trial's end beside thee, that Love's incarnate rose I yet may know--

Again, Yours, Billy."

The words float over the bustle of the "War Room". The clerks came and went, delivering stacks of papers for Capulet and carrying away new armfuls of documents for review. Horatio scowled at anyone who came near his corner of the room where he guarded the ledgers he kept of the trial teams accounts, where he closely guarded the master lists of documents they would review more closely, and where he kept deposition scripts they hoped soon to unleash on the Danish King and his groundskeepers.

"Another round of ales!" Capulet might bark without warning. Or, just as likely, he might rouse himself from his chair and shout: "Flavius! We are in need of a miracle, m'Boy!"

But the footage shows that Capulet was not the man running the case—it was Billy who took command. Capulet was their leader, their financier, and their chief strategist. But it was Billy who saw to it that the clerks were fed; it was Billy who saw to it that the deposition schedule was kept. And it was Billy who leaned on Flavius daily to pull a miracle from the thick air of Belgium...er, the Netherlands.

"Tell me truly, Flavius, on what dost thou toil?" Billy flipped through the book at Flavius's side, but could make no sense of it.

"'Tis a code of civil procedure, Bill," Flavius said, but did not look up from the book he was nose-deep inside. "The procedure of courts most distant that do press for justice in far China."

"And this? *The Corpus Juris Civilis*? By Jove, Man! This is the Code of Emperor Justinian!"[15]

"'Tis," Flavius said. Again he did not look up.

"By the laws of the Mongols, the laws of the Chinese. By the code of the Empire of the Greeks. You do labour so!" Billy said.

"Yet I find nothing. I find nothing!"

Capulet struggled to cross the room and muscled his way into the their conversation.

---

[15] **Editor's Note:** The *Corpus Juris Civilis* was a vast code of laws compiled by Emperor Justinian in an attempt to organize the laws of the Roman Empire.

"What news?"

"No news, Lord Capulet," Flavius answered. He dropped the book and leaned back in his chair. He rubbed his face and then scratched at his crotch before standing to stretch. "There is no *news*, for there is no law to support this…this…lawyers' folly."

Capulet sighed and leaned against the table.

"Make it—"

"Nay," Flavius interrupted. "Nay," he said again, and then picked up one of his thick legal volumes and threw it across the room. "NAY!" he shouted.

"Flavius," Billy shouted. He put his hand on Flavius's shoulder. "Calm thyself."

"You ask the impossible!" Flavius shouted.

"No," Capulet corrected. He smiled. "We ask *only* the impossible. And we ask it only of thee, Flavius."

Just then the big doors opened. Prince Hamlet stood framed in the light of the door. He was a spindly thing, svelte and waifish, who seemed to be asking the breeze to knock him over.

"Young master Hamlet!" Capulet called out. He smiled and went limping across the room toward his client. "We were just discussing your case! Flavius here tells us that we've got them dead to rights."

"Oh do you?" Hamlet asked. He looked down, away from Capulet. Hamlet was often afraid of making eye contact. He pushed a soft wisp of hair out of his eyes, then pushed it back in front of his eyes.

"Come meet your team," Capulet said. He led the young Prince through the jumbled War Room and introduced the Prince first to the clerks, then to Horatio, then to Flavius, and finally to Billy Shakespeare.

"And this, Good Prince, is my Second Chair. Willy *the Bodkin* Shakespeare."

"You're the good Englishman who did write me so," Hamlet cooed.

"I am," Shakespeare said. He nodded and bowed. "'Tis an honor to finally meet you, Your Highness."

"Oh, he said *Your Highness!*" Hamlet said, and giggled. "Your words cut me, Shakespeare. They cut me. Like…like a knife."

"I did not mean the Good Prince harm."

"Your words made me *feel* again," Hamlet said. "Like a knife."

"Yes. Well, not *quite* sure that I follow thy words, Your Highness."

"OH! You said it again! He said *Your Highness* again. But call me Hamlet, Billy Shakes. *Do* call me Hamlet. It makes me…*feel.*"

"Yes…well," Shakespeare said. He looked to Capulet for assistance, but Capulet shook his head and shrugged. "It was our pleasure to aid you with your troubles legal."

"And did you get the payment that I sent you?"

"Well, that's enough of this talk!" Capulet interrupted. "Good Prince, if you would be so kind, I'd like to talk with you about your testimony in some place more private. I've a great deal of *coaching* that I'd like to do."

"I'd like that. I'm awfully nervous," the Prince said. He took a step back as if he were going to leave, but then stepped toward Shakespeare and put his hand on Shakespeare's shoulder. "I said that you made me feel again."

"Yes, Good Prince. Glad to be of service."

The Prince then floated away and Capulet followed.

"Did you bloody well see that?" Shakespeare asked.

"He's a strange demon!" Flavius laughed.

"He smells of oranges and rose petals," Shakespeare said. "He wouldn't even look me in the eyes!"

"He's a *writer*!" Flavius said and laughed. He slapped Billy on the shoulder. "I told you about accepting the custom of writers!"

"Nay," Shakespeare said. He was now smiling, too. "*I* am a writer. *He* is a *novelist*. Back to work, everyone!"

Our story then faded out, fading back in at some undetermined later time. It was dark outside, the clerks had gone home, and only Shakespeare remained in the War Room. Capulet entered from the large doors, and Shakespeare looked up from his folio.

"You need sleep," Capulet called out across the room.

"No," Billy answered. "I labor this night on matters private."

"Your plays?"

"Yes," Billy answered. "But in truth no. It's only just a sonnet. For Anne."

Capulet limped in, his steps resounding in the now empty room. He sat near Shakespeare and offered a bottle of the *porto*. Billy took a glass.

"About the payment that young Hamlet referenced," Capulet said.

"Yes, about that."

"Are you sure you want to know?"

"Yes," Shakespeare said.

"It was a sketch. As payment, he sent a sketch—a *drawing*. I say this in seriousness. A sketch on paper of the Good Prince, himself, naked. With a dead cat. He was beside a pond in the sketch. They were having a picnic. Beneath it he wrote, 'To be or not to be, cat is the question.' I thought that this news might make you uncomfortable."

"Our client is a fucking loon," Billy said. He coughed and then drank from his glass. Capulet had not stopped smiling.

"Yes. Yes, he is. I promise thee, Will, I knew not of his mental condition when I accepted his retainer."

"He's a mad as a fecking hatter, he is."

"Aye," Capulet agreed. "But he has been wronged."

"Bacon will crucify him on the stand."

"Nonsense, Will. Hamlet's a loon. But he's royalty. He'll be strong as on ox on that stand. It's bred into them. My mother's family was prominent in Wales, did I ever tell you that?"

"You mentioned it, Sir."

"Yes. Very prominent. We are *Welsh* royalty—if there be such a thing. We descend from King Arthur! If Welsh blood can carry a royal worth through the eons, then my blood does carry that pomp and vigor. As does the blood in Hamlet's veins."

"My family ate shit and worked in mines, Sir. I'm sorry if I don't share your respect for the royal classes."

"Respect?" Capulet laughed. "Hah. Your words go to far. Respect is not the word for the passion that I feel toward young Hamlet, nor toward Claudius. Nor, indeed, toward my own kin. We are a different breed, though. We are a different thing."

The cameras moved away. Hamlet and Capulet seemed to be deep inside a large cavern, far away from the world. Capulet smiled, but his words and his brow were heavy.

"Well. Now is as good a time as any to tell you. Claudius will not be deposed."

"Of course not," Billy said. He finished his *porto*. "Why would anything work in our favor?"

"His Kingly schedule simply won't allow it, he says. I am afraid that we cannot compel him. But he *will* be at the trial."

"The groundskeepers, Sir?"

"Those depositions will take place as planned," Capulet said. "And much depends upon them, as does much depend on…everything, really. Much always depends upon everything."

"Perhaps 'tis you who needs sleep, Sir."

"Willy. Willy, Willy. Willy the Bodkin Shakes. We are not two weeks from a moment that will, I am afraid, define our lives from now to the end of us."

There was a tenderness in the moment, almost a father-son quality about the two men sitting in the darkness. Shakespeare broke the silence:

"Cap. I want you to know, that no matter what happens, I shall not blame thee. 'Twas my decision to join this fool's errand."

Capulet stood immediately and began limping away.

"Nonsense, Willy!" he said as he walked out of the room. "Nonsense. We'll all be rich this time next month. Get some sleep, Willy Shakes. We are such stuff as dreams are made on, after all."

EPISODE 15:

St. David's Day

CAPULET'S WAR ROOM IN THE HAGUE was a hectic, crowded space. The War Room operated at full speed 24 hours a day. The windows and the walls were stained from the soot of candles and whale oil lamps. Capulet, Billy, and Flavius worked 20-hour days and Horatio worked almost as much. The clerks kept slightly better hours, but ran around in a hectic, un-choreographed dance in the background.[16]

Capulet had also taken on two Brussels-based contract attorneys, although no one knew how he was financing the project. Apparently they were being paid hourly. The Belgian contract attorneys tried very hard to "be a part of the team" and to pitch in, and they spent long hours in the War Room along with Capulet's British men. But the Brussels-based contract attorneys spoke Flemish, so no one ever knew what they were saying. Flavius sent them out for drinks frequently.

---

[16] **Editor's Note:** The raw footage from this period is astoundingly boring. I'd like to thank the director of the film for doing such tight cutting and editing—there are literally hundreds of hours of footage where nothing happens except maybe one of the clerks farts. The finished Episode 14, called "St. David's Day", is really a masterpiece, though. You'd think that everything in a trial preparation was dramatic and exciting if this was all you had to base it on.

"Which of us did the deposition work? Hear ye!" Horatio shouted over the buzz of the War Room. "I ask which of us did the deposition work?"

"*I* took them each in league with Cap and Will. What of it?" Flavius answered back. Tempers ran very short in the War Room.

"No!" Horatio shouted back. "I mean *the argument*! You think I don't know who took the depositions?"

"What? What the hell are you even talking about?" Flavius asked.

"The argument of course! The argument about the testimony of the late king, of course! I've lost my copy of the brief."

"What do you need it for?" Flavius asked.

"Flavius, I swear. Do you have an extra or not?" Horatio shot back. He stood and shook his tiny fist at Flavius. "I must review the evidentiary rules on spectral testimony—Cap wants the rules in note form to review before argument."

"Why *then* did you not phrase your question in terms of the evidentiary rules?"

"What else would I ask of you!?" Horatio shouted. "I'm sorry...I didn't realize that you had only joined the trial team this morning. Did you not know that the entire trial hangs on spectral testimony? Well, perhaps we should just step back a moment and I can give you a sort of overview of the case from 10,000 feet—just so we're on the same page."

Horatio was extremely agitated. But a smile grew across Flavius's face, and it became clear that he'd been having a go with Horatio.

"They are here, Ass," Flavius laughed. He held up a roughly bound stack of papers for Horatio to see.

"You are the ass who knows not what rides on today. Give 'em t'me when I ask ye for 'em next time."

"Watch your tongue with me. I—"

"Would you both shut up?" Billy shouted. "We are on the same team. We are all very tired. Flavius, hand over your extra copy of the brief. Don't pretend you didn't know what he asked of you. My God. It's like babysitting."

"Am I in the wrong, *M'Lord*?" Flavius asked Billy.

"No, I am *not* a Lord," Billy answered. "I hear your tone. And it is *true* that I am also an associate. True. But today I am, regrettably, your boss. We are all suffering, Flavius, for wont of help. I know as well as you both know that we've each done the work of four men. And the clerks have thrice threatened to quit us and away back to England. Horatio—who has molested you constantly this hour last— has not slept in four days. Know I this for I have not slept in *five* days. Let us please be patient with one another and save our anger for Claudius and his counsel or, barring that, Montague and his men—they sit idle in Birmingham while we slave. Capulet even in the last moment unto this trial begged his assistance and Montague denied it us. I ask you both, please do not yell anymore, rather save that passion, as I have, and dedicate it to wishing assistance from Montague—"

Just then Capulet entered the room loudly through the big swinging oak doors. Each of the arguing attorneys in the room fell silent in deference to Capulet.

"What's he that wishes so?" Capulet asked, and a smile grew on his face. He limped across the room to the long table the attorneys shared. "My cousin, Will Shakespeare? No, my fair cousin: If we are mark'd to lose this trial, we are enough to do our client loss; and if to win, the fewer men, the greater contingency share! God's Will! I pray thee, wish not one man more! God's peace! I would not lose so great an honour as one man more, methinks, would share from me for the best hope I have."

The clerks, who had been silently and slavishly working in the background stepped forward, the better to hear Capulet speak.

"O! Do not wish one more! Rather proclaim it, Will Shakespeare, as my host, that he which hath no stomach to this trial, let him depart; his passport shall be made. And crowns for convoy put into his purse! We would not litigate in that man's company that fears his fellowship to litigate with us."

Capulet seemed to consider sitting at the table, but then, seeing the clerks gather round, he rather stood up as straight as he could. He leaned against the table and addressed the whole room:

"This day is called the feast of our St. David. He that argues this day, and comes safe home, will stand a tip-toe when the day is named, and rouse him at the name of St. David. He that argues this day, and see old age, will yearly on the vigil meet his accountants and say 'Tomorrow is Saint David's Day:' Then will he strip his accounts and ledgers and say, 'These pounds I had on David's Day.' Old men forget: yet all shall be forgot, but he'll remember—with advantages—arguments made that day. Then shall our names, familiar in his mouth as household words, Lord Capulet, Will Shakes and Flavius, Horatio, those clerks over there, be in their flowing cups freshly rememb'red. This story shall good law schools teach students and Davy David shall ne'er go by, from this day to the ending of the world, but we in it shall be remember'd. We few, we happy few, we firm of partners; for he today that argues with me shall be my partner. Be he ne'er so vile, this day shall gentle his condition! Montague and them in England now a-bed shall think themselves accursed they were not here, and hold their manhoods cheap whiles any speaks that litigated with us upon Saint David's Day!"

A great wave of cheering and shouting rose up from the assembled attorneys. They shouted "Hear! Hear!" and "We'll be *rich!*" And then, just as Capulet's entry had ended Will's and Flavius's argument, a knock on those large oak doors stopped the attorneys' jubilation.

"Who knocks?" Capulet asked. Horatio jogged to the door and opened it.

"'Tis Montjoy the herald, Sir!" Horatio answered. "Perhaps they've agreed to settle on our terms."

Montjoy was a tall man built like a flagpole. He entered the room proudly, walking tall with a smooth gait.

"Capulet," Montjoy said. He presented himself in front of Capulet with a bow and he removed his hat with a regal flourish. "Once more I come to know of thee, Capulet, if for a ransom thou wilt now compound, before thy most assured overthrow; for certainly thy client is so near the gulf, thou needs must be englutted. Besides, in mercy, Sir Bacon desires thee thou wilt mind thy followers of repentance; that their souls may make a peaceful and sweet retire from this court, where, wretches, their poor careers must lie and fester."

Capulet listened to the herald's remarks and his face betrayed not a single emotion. His team gathered behind him, falling into rank behind Capulet and then behind Will Shakespeare and Flavius.

"Thou dost thy office fairly," Capulet said. He turned briefly and looked over his assembled team, then turned back to the herald. "Turn thee back. And tell Bacon I do not seek him now; but could be willing to argue to verdict without impeachment; for, to say the sooth, though 'tis no wisdom to confess so much unto an enemy of craft and vantage, my lawyers are with sickness much enfeebled, my numbers lessened, and those few I have almost no better than so many French. And so, Montjoy, fare you well. The sum of all our answer is but this: We would not seek a trial, as we are; nor, as we are, we say we will not shun it: So tell your master."

The response surprised Montjoy a bit at first, but then he nodded calmly and said: "I shall deliver so. Thanks to you, Lord Capulet." Montjoy left the room and a heavy silence fell over Capulet's War Room.[17]

---

[17] **Editor's Note:** Wow. This director is really getting lazy. Here the episode fades to black and fades back in presumably much later on that night. In point of fact, it seems that he decided to leave out almost a whole week of trial preparation. When the episode comes back, it is late at night in the War Room on the night before the trial. Will and the team are arguing—yet again!—about the testimony of the late king.

It's really a shame that they cut out that week, because it was an important week. The clerks all quit. They quit because they had no faith whatsoever that the Capulet team would win. They had been struggling for several months to put together a good case and had pretty much failed. So the clerks bolted.

Capulet's men were back to work in the next instant.

"We'll never get his testimony in," Flavius said. "There is simply no way."

"We'll get it in," Capulet coughed. He had deep blue bags under his eyes by this time.

"Sir, with respect, I've been through the volumes front to back, and I've found nary an example of a magistrate allowing such." Flavius dropped his quill on the table and leaned back in his chair in resignation. They'd brought him on the team for this one reason—the evidentiary matter. And he'd failed.

"Did you look in *all* the jurisdictions?" Billy asked.

"Of course, Bill," Flavius said.

"And in the treatises?" Capulet asked.

Flavius held up a massive, loosely bound treatise on evidence.

"Sir, of course I did." Flavius dropped the book on the table with a loud bang. "Magistrate Smith's treatise, *On the Admissibility of Spectral Testimony,* which is considered the leading work on the

---

Also, Will got a very important letter in the mail from Anne. She wrote to him about one of his plays! In the letter, she made a few rather harsh suggestions about a play of his that he had originally titled "Much Ado About Sexual Congress". It was an important letter, but the director just cut it out entirely. This director is always talking a big game in the background about how "unfair" Elizabethan society was, but then he goes and cuts out one of the most important parts of the story! Why? I don't know. I guess I'll ask him in three hundred years. This is a frustrating project.

Anyway, the episode fades back up on the team assembled around the table under the light of a few candles and a whale oil lamp. Thankfully, the director cut out several hours of discussion about the pros and cons of the whale oil industry.

matter. The law is clear, Sir, that spectral testimony is inadmissible when offered to prove the truth of the matter asserted by the horrible spectre."

"Yes, but there are exceptions," Capulet said.

"Yes, Sir. The well-developed exceptions that we have been over and *over* a thousand times. But I have been through the case law, Sir—and may I remind you, again, that I was adjunct at Oxford and taught under Magistrate Smith on the rules of evidence. There simply is no exception that will cover the testimony of a dead King's spectre visiting his son to tell of his own death, much less to name his own murderer! We deal not with a business record, nor with an excited utterance!"

No one spoke for many moments. Capulet turned from the group and almost toward the camera. He whispered to himself: "All is lost. All is lost."

Flavius adjusted the stack of research in front of him, as if that might help, and they each waited to hear the inevitable announcement from Capulet that all was lost. But then, Billy spoke up.

"Flavius...when did the King die?"

Flavius shook his head as if the question wasn't worth answering, but he thumbed through the stack of papers in front of him.

"Night time," he answered. "March 15th, Will."

"And when interred?"

"End of month, I think. March 31st. Why?" Flavius asked.

"In your research, Flavius, and in your teaching at Oxford..."

"Ponce College," Capulet said, and turned back to the group. Billy laughed and then leaned closer to the table.

"Have you found any well-reasoned opinion establishing when exactly the eternal soul of a Believer ascends unto Heaven to resideth unto the Lord?"[18]

"Nay, verily. Of course not, Will," Flavius answered. "'Tis an ecclesiastical matter at best, at worst a question of fact to be found by a jury. 'Twould not appear in a statement from the bench."

"So how can we be certain when the Good Soul of the King did depart for the Elysian Fields?"

"Well, I—"

"I mean, obviously it did not ascend immediately, or 'twould not have lingered about to haunt poor Hamlet, so."

"I fail to see the point of your...." Flavius said, but then he stopped talking. Slowly at first he began to smile. "My Word."

"Yes?" Capulet asked. "Am I missing it?"

"Dying declaration, Sir," Flavius said. "Boddy Shakes is a genius! 'Tis the chief exception to the rule excluding spectral testimony. Such evidence, when given upon the deathbed, is considered to be reliable—for the dying Christian is merely trying to cleanse his eternal spark before baptism in life eternal among the choir invisible. Res ipsa loquitur, Sir."

---

[18] **Editor's Note:** There are a lot of close ups in this section. I think the director is trying to show that they were each, individually, coming to a realization about a potential loophole in the laws of evidence regarding spectral testimony. The technique of using tight portrait shots to show realization works very dramatically in this scene. In fact, it works so well that a casual viewer might get the idea that this type of group realization actually happens, where attorneys all come to the same logical conclusion at the same time. This never actually happens, though. In the real world, lawyers very rarely agree on anything and almost never come to realizations at the same time...about anything.

"Ponce talk. What the hell does that mean?"

"The thing speaks for itself, Sir," Flavius answered. "If we can show that the King's soul did not ascend to Heaven immediate, which we surely can on Hamlet's own testimony and on the testimony of those plebe groundskeeepers, then we have therefore already proven that the King's soul was not yet dead. He walked among us, Sir, though in the form of a horrible spectre."

"By Jove!" Capulet shouted.

"Yes, Sir. Exactly, Sir! By Jove the King na'er appeared again unto this Earthly clime after his counsel with his son—therefore, he must have been in that very instant in the throes of soul-death!"

"God's Peace! This is mad, mad stupidity! It's crazy!" Capulet shouted.

"Yes, M'Lord," Flavius agreed. Then turned to the camera. "So crazy that it just might—"

"We are fucking awesome," Capulet interrupted. "Horatio! To your quill pen!"

Horatio scribbled maniacally as Hamlet and Flavius argued out the finer points of the argument that they would make. Meanwhile, Hamlet's voice came over the scene, reading from his latest letter to his dear Anne:

My Dearest Anne:
I did not know thy spirit's injury,
Nor that I did wield injurious blade.
And if your words in truth describe your course,
I yield to it the passions of my own.
If saints reside in the Heavenly House,

Or darker demons beneath our trodding,

Of them both I beg an immortal's strength

To end my life's one hard resolution

And kill my solemn infatuation

Which did impede your life: My love, my greed.

Did not for praise or flattery believe

This wretched thing that one so fair could love.

Good faith, I now propose a fair custom,

To trade your nightmare of my creation.

Be free of it and, on my life, of me,

And my Life's Ransom on the barrelhead.

I shall write thee no more.

Ever, Your Friend, William Shakespeare.

Episode 16:

We Call Hamlet

THE SOUTHERN WALL OF THE VAST COURTROOM[19] was tall glass windows to let in as much sunlight as possible. Still, it was not so bright in the courtroom as it could have been, and the darkness made all the men in the courtroom glow like dull, morose lawyers. Their robes and wigs did little to help. The magistrate sat upon a very high bench with his back nearly turned to the camera. Seven men sat in the jury box. The plaintiff, Hamlet, and the defendant, Claudius, each sat with their attorneys at benches in front of the judge. Hamlet was a very thin young man with a soft wisp of hair that fell over his forehead and covered one eye. His clothes were very tight.

Capulet rose.

"If it please the Court, We call Hamlet, Prince of Denmark."

Hamlet rose from his seat and approached the bench.

---

[19] **Editor's Note:** My apologies, but this episode just opens directly in the courtroom. I feel like the director may have been running on a deadline or maybe had just lost interest in the project and wanted it done as soon as possible, so instead of setting up the story or giving us a review of what's happened in the last episode, he just blasts right into a courtroom scene. Just, 'BANG! We call Hamlet!' practically.

"As is your right, Prince, would you prefer testimony on oath or by ordeal?"

"Oath, I'd say," Hamlet answered.

"Do you swear to tell the truth, the whole truth, and nothing but the truth, so help you GOD?"

"I so swear," Hamlet swore.

"State your name."

"Well, I'm Hamlet."

"And your occupation?" Capulet asked.

"What do you mean?"

"What do you *do*?"

"Novelist," Hamlet answered.

"Yes, I think we're all aware of that. But what do you do for income?"

"Oh, well I'm the Prince of Denmark, which, until recently, had been quite lucrative."

"And where were you on the 15th of this March past?"[20]

"Traveling. Brussels, Brittany, all around the Continent, really. Doing research for my novel."[21]

---

[20] **Editor's Note:** Here, the director lost interest in the fixed camera aesthetic that he'd initially had with the courtroom scene. Instead, the cameraman, who is presumably the director himself, walked freely around the courtroom. The result is to make the scene *feel* as if the wheels of justice were really in motion. My interns all agree that this change in cinematography really made this scene "pop".

[21] **Editor's Note:** Hamlet's novel was never finished during the filming of this reality program. In point of fact, it was not a novel at all, but a "memoir" called *Heartbreaking Work of Staggering Genius*. That Hamlet never finished his memoir is likely a good thing, given that all evidence indicates that Hamlet was an

"And on the 15th of that same month?" Capulet asked.

"Traveling."

"And when didst thou returneth to Castle Elsinore?"

"Oh, it was May, I believe."

"And upon arrival, did you not speak to the groundskeepers?"

"I did."

"And did they not tell you news that the spectral apparition of your father was at that very moment haunting Castle Elsinore?" Capulet asked.

"They did."

Capulet limped toward the bench of His Honor, the Magistrate, while carrying a single piece of paper in his hand.

"Your honor, may I approach the witness?" The Magistrate nodded and Capulet approached Hamlet. "Hamlet, could you identify for the good Christian men of the jury what this paper is?"

---

awful writer. On the other hand, his failure to finish his *Heartbreaking Work of Staggering Genius* would eventually send horrid, awful repercussions waffling out through space and time, as this failure indirectly opened the gates for Dave Eggers's work of the same title a few hundred years later. What I am about to reveal to you is, strictly speaking, beyond the scope of this novella, but my interns read and abridged *The Authorized True and Completely Reliable History of Western Civilization*, which you might recall was also accidentally dropped from the time machine, and discovered that after the fall of the United States, and after a period of anarcho-syndicalism in the western hemisphere, global capitalistic order is re-established by a sect of neo-Christian royalists who base their theology primarily on that *Duck Dynasty* family. There is born one young man named Saul who might rise to challenge the authoritarian *Duck Dynasty* regime. However, Saul is killed as a young man when a copy Eggers's memoir falls off a library shelf and strikes Saul in the head, just as he is beginning his rise as a liberator. The consequences will be dire.

"Yes. 'Tis a page ripped from my official appointments registry, from this May 15th passed."

"And could you read what it says around 3:30 that afternoon?"

"Yes. 'Counsel w/Father.' Clearly," Hamlet answered.

"Thank you. If it please the Court, this will be entered as Plaintiff's Exhibit A."

Capulet handed the document to the jury. Then he presented to Hamlet a roughly bound book.

"Good Prince, could you now explain to the Jury what book I did present to you?"

"Yes. This is the rest of my appointments registry from this passed March until today, this March 1. It's a standard thing, really, the Crown Secretary prepares it."

"And could you flip through that book and identify for all of us when was the date of your next counsel with your father's spectral apparition?"

"Why, no, Counselor. Of course not," Hamlet answered.

"And why not?"

"Well I could flip through until day endeth, but there was only one meeting with my Father."

"Oh, my mistake. Why was that?"

"Well, because upon termination thereof he did ascend unto Heaven to sitteth among the choir invisible."

"Oh, yes," Capulet said. He tapped at his chest with the book in his good hand. "My mistake. Your Honor, Plaintiff's Exhibit B?" The Magistrate nodded and Capulet handed the book to the jury. "Prince Hamlet, when you took Earthly counsel with the spectral apparition of your father, did he recount to you…"[22] Capulet paused. "Did the spectral apparition of your father recount to you…the nature of his bodily demise?"

"OBJECTION!" Sir Francis Bacon shouted as he leapt up from his seat behind the defendant's table. "This is hearsay, your honor!"

"Your Honor, by your leave, the nature of his bodily demise is not in question before the Court. I admit I know not why Bacon would object so."

The Magistrate stroked his chin and the locks of his ridiculous white wig.

"I'll allow it," The Magistrate said. "But watch yourself, Capulet."

"Yes, Sir. Of course, Sir. Do answer, Good Prince."

"He did," Hamlet answered.

"And what was the nature of his bodily demise?"

"'Twas murder," Hamlet answered.

"OBJECTION!" Bacon shouted. "Your Honor?"

The Magistrate thought, stroked his chin and the white wig.

"I'll allow it. But watch yourself, Capulet."

"Of course, Your Honor." Capulet inhaled deeply and, with his back to the judge, showed a secret thumbs-up sign to Billy.

"Prince Hamlet. When you did take Earthly counsel with the spectral apparition of your father, did he then convey unto you…" He paused again, still unsure whether he should go forward. He

---

[22] **Editor's Note:** Here, Capulet paused for a bit. The director did quite a good job on this scene getting across that Capulet was, even at that last moment, unsure whether he should go forward with his line of questioning.

looked to his table for assurance and Billy nodded to him. "Did he then convey unto you the identity of his murderer?"

"OBJECTION, YOUR HONOR!" Bacon shouted. Now he leapt not only out of his chair, but strode angrily into the center of the courtroom. "This is spectral hearsay by the textbook! Or would be, if we used textbooks! He's attempting to establish the identity of the King's murderer by the spectral testimony of the King himself."

"Your Honor?" Capulet asked. He smiled and shrugged his good shoulder as if there was nothing at all wrong with his question. "But I can hardly call the Late King himself, can I? If Bacon would prefer, perhaps we should recess until such time that Your Honor might call a coven of witches to summon the Late King from his eternal slumber? We'd all be here until the next solstice!"

The good men of the jury laughed out loud.

"This is a travesty and an offense!" Bacon objected.

"Your Honor, we readily admit that this testimony seems at first blush to be barred by the general rule excluding spectral testimony as hearsay. But, as I am sure your wise and learned honor is aware, there are a number of well-developed exceptions to the general rule. Chief among them, for our purposes, is the exception for dying declarations—"

"Dying declaration!?" Bacon laughed. "He'd been in the ground a month, Capulet!"

Here, Capulet gave just about the most amazing performance you could ever imagine. He put a look of overwhelming confusion on his face.

"Yes, well, obvious his Christian soul had not yet departed for Elysian Fields, else he wouldn't have been bantering about the castle bothering anyone who would lend him an ear. 'Tis clear that his soul lingered on until taking counsel with the Prince, upon which he ascended unto his eternal commission. I really don't see the controversy here, Your Honor?"

The Magistrate thought a long time on it. He stroked his chin and then stroked his powdered white whig.

"I'll allow it. But watch yourself, Capulet."

"Of course, Your Honor. Go on, Prince Hamlet."

"He did convey unto me such identity," Hamlet answered.

"And when you took that Earthly counsel with the spectral apparition of your bodily departed father, whom did he name as his slayer?"

Hamlet stood and pointed at his uncle Claudius.

"'Twas his brother, Claudius, who does now sitteth in this very courtroom."

Everyone in the courtroom hrrmphed.[23]

"The Plaintiff now terminates our direct examination, Your Honor," Capulet said.

Capulet limped proudly back to his table. Billy smiled and was proud and happy.

---

[23] **Editor's Note:** Ok, this is just utter nonsense. At this point in the episode, you can hear everyone in the courtroom saying 'Hrrmph hrrmph hrrmph.' But that never happened; the director added that hrrmph noise in post-production. I've looked at the raw footage, and the scene was actually quite stoic and quiet in reality. The addition of the hrrmph track certainly adds to the drama of the subject, but it does little to preserve the actual historical record. It's pandering, you know—just like you see on reality TV programs.

But Sir Bacon was quickly up out of his chair and walked quickly toward Hamlet.

"Cross, Your Honor?" Bacon asked. The Magistrate nodded. "Hamlet—"

"*You forget yourself, Sir,*" Hamlet corrected him.

"My apologies. *Prince* Hamlet. Beg your leave. When you took Earthly counsel with the spectral apparition of your departed father, did he by any chance tell you the *manner* of his bodily demise?"

"OBJECTION!" Capulet shouted. "Your Honor, relevance?"

Without missing a beat, The Magistrate said: "I'll allow it. But watch yourself, Bacon."

"Of course, Your Honor. Prince?"

"He did," Hamlet said.

"And what was the nature of his demise? Beyond murder, I mean. By what means was his finish accomplished?"

"Claudius did set upon him while he slept," Hamlet said.

"And? By what means did the spectral apparition allege that death was unto him wielded?"

"OBJECTION! Relevance?" Horatio called out. Flavius restrained Horatio, pulled him back into his seat and whispered into his ear.

Hamlet went on, "Claudius did pour a noxious poison unto my Father's ear."

"In his *ear!*" Bacon repeated and laughed. "In his EAR?! Well, first time hearing everything, I suppose. Is that a *common* means of consummating regal fratricide?" Bacon asked.

"Objection, Your Honor," Flavius said, and stood. "Calls for speculation. Hamlet has not been called as an expert on regal fratricide."

The Magistrate raised his hand to rub his chin, but then stopped.

"Yes, that one's actually going to be sustained, I think."

"Withdrawn, Your Honor," Bacon said and laughed. He roamed the courtroom aimlessly for a moment, and Hamlet looked confused.

"Prince Hamlet…if you would be so kind, could you tell the Court of your current state of health?"

"I'm quite fit, I'd say. I usually run of a morning and I've four dressage horses that I work during the day. Keeps me active, gets me out in the open air."

"Yes, and what of your mental health?"

"Objection," Capulet said. "Relevance, your honor?"

"Goes to the credibility of the witness, Your Honor," Sir Francis Bacon said.

"I'll allow it. But watch yourself, Bacon."

"Of course, Your Honor."

"Your Honor," Capulet said. "My client is not on trial here."

"I said I will allow it, Capulet. Hold thy tongue."

Bacon turned back to Hamlet and went on: "Please tell us, Good Prince, what of your current mental health?"

"Everyone gets a little down sometimes, Counselor. Especially after the death of one's father. I suppose I've suffered a bit of melancholy this past year."

Bacon collected a page from the defendant's table and held it up as he walked back to Hamlet and handed it to him.

"Good Prince, is it not true that on account of this 'melancholy', as you called it, you have thrice weekly sought treatment from the Crown's Office of Exorcism Emotional?"

Hamlet paused and looked at Capulet for guidance, but Capulet only nodded.

"Please answer the question."

"Everyone gets down sometimes."

Bacon handed the paper to Hamlet.

"Your Honor, with your permission, this is a report from the Crown's Office of Exorcism Emotional regarding young Hamlet's current sanity."

"OBJECTION!" Capulet shouted and again tried to stand. "Your Honor, this is the first we've heard of this. Why were we not apprised of such evidence ahead of time? And who call they to attest veracity thereof?"

"Your Honor," Bacon answered. "Where is the rule that the defendants must have access to our trial materials? That's liberal-progressive nonsense. Anyway, we ourselves were apprised of this only this very morning. As for the document, it is a government document, attested under Seal of the Crown, just as was the Prince's appointments registry."

"I'll allow it," the Magistrate said. "I want to see where this is going."

"Thank you, Your Honor. Prince, could you read the document for us."

Hamlet exhaled deeply and rubbed his brow. He was embarrassed.

"Patient is a crown-prince, heir-apparent to the throne of Denmark; he shows remarkable imagination and a gift for storytelling as demonstrated by his recent series of short stories published—"

"*Lower*, Good Prince. Please skip right to the conclusion. Right there, bottom paragraph."

"Hamlet is crazy as shit and has seven demons upon his frontal lobe," Hamlet said.

"The defense rests."

The screen faded to black, then faded in.[24]

The Magistrate called out, "We'll now hear closing argument. Bacon, you won the krone toss so you first."

"Thank you, Your Honor," Bacon said. He rose and began his swagger around the courtroom. "Gentlemen of the Jury, something is rotten in the state of Denmark, and you need look no further than this courtroom to see it. You sit in judgment of an honourable man, yet you Danes sit here in The Hague. Know ye why? Because at this very moment in Denmark, the dockets are bloated with imaginative actions and frivolous torts. I, for one, apologize to you that we've commanded so much of your time on such a fancy pursuit as this spoiled brat's greedy quest to quench his Princely thirst. This trial

---

[24] **Editor's Note:** Well, thankfully, the director cut out several procedural motions here. There were about three hours of the lawyers going back and forth on procedural matters that would bore the socks off of even the most dedicated litigator. In place of these procedural matters, the director did another fade-out/fade-in. Too easy, I'd say. He could have cut to an interview with Billy or with Capulet, or something, and built tension like they do in modern day reality TV shows. But that's just my opinion.

has been a farce. Capulet has tried to arouse in you your vengeful passions based upon what? Not based upon evidence, surely, for he's presented us no proof short of the ravings of a depraved Prince and the imaginative tale of a departed King. No, his case is based not on proof, but upon a story. A tale told by an idiot, full of sound and fury, but, alas, signifying nothing. I know that you will all do the right thing—the right thing for Denmark—and return verdict of not guilty and refuse to entertain the pleadings of this gluttonous, literary Prince. Thank you."

Bacon re-took his chair at the defendant's table and Claudius shook his hand. They were quite proud of themselves and it looked pretty clear that they had the case wrapped up.

"Lord Capulet," the Magistrate said and motioned at Capulet's table. "Want to give it a shot?"

Capulet stood and limped toward the jury. He could not swagger like Bacon swaggered, but he didn't *try* to swagger like Bacon, either. It looked as though he may have been playing up his deformity.

"You'll not hear this often from a barrister, but I am at a loss for words: a loss of words to describe what we have seen in this courtroom today; for who among us can describe how demons do turn the hearts of good Christian men when gold and power are in play? Begging your pardon, Good Christian Men of the Jury, I apologize to you. I am not from Denmark, nor would I presume to pontificate upon the government justly apportioned there. But, if the people of Denmark are anything like the people of Birmingham, where I live, then you know a wronged man when you see one, and a wicked man when you see one; you know a justice when you see one, and an injustice when you see one. You have heard a story today of a

just man wronged by the injustice of a wicked man. 'Tis a shame.
King Claudius was likely a just man in his youth, as were we all, but
in his ambition, he went mad. Lust. Lust for gold, and lust for the
Good Queen did drive his passions to drive him, and he did set upon
and slay his very own brother. We were all in the same courtroom
today, so I have very little doubt but that you will return a verdict of
guilty as to the murder. No one could mistake that. But that's not
really why we're here today, is it? I've come before you not begging a
King's justice, nor even a Prince's justice—no. I've come begging
you for a son's justice. 'Tis on this account that I beg your pardon, for
I am forced now to ask you to defile and to debase your own
conscience."

Capulet took frequent breaks to take deep breaths and look deep
in thought.

"Were this a perfect world, I would ask that upon your verdict of
guilty you would command the resurrection of the late King, so that
he might once again embrace his son and his wife. But that is not
within our power. The King will not return from his eternal
commission. 'Tis the great injustice of the World that good Christian
men are often powerless to put straight what has been made crooked
by the ambitions of wicked men. And if that be the bar you set, then
we will all fail, for the King is dead, and he is not coming back.

"Forgive me—I lost my own father when I was scarce younger
than my friend, Hamlet. So I know a bit of the heart that beats in his
chest in this moment. And I know that from this day to the end of
Hamlet, not a day will pass but in it Hamlet will pray one more
moment with his father, to tell him what his fatherhood meant, so that
his father may look proudly upon him. My dear Hamlet, that never

shall happen. That hole in your heart will never be filled. Good Jury, whether you award a pound or a kingdom, Hamlet's soul will never be full again, and his heart will never stop beating for the memory of his slain father. Yet Bacon says that I am here, in this Court, to ask you to replace this boy's father with petty coins? No. I would never.

"Alas, we have but one crude tool in this matter with which to dispense justice. 'Tis this account I beg your pardon asking you to defile your conscience and make such substitution. Not for a King's justice, nor even a Prince's justice for a stolen crown, but for a son's justice. The King is dead, and we cannot resurrect him, for we do not have that in our power. Hamlet's father is dead, and we cannot resurrect him, for we do not have that in our power. But we are empowered by the Lord to commit this man's soul to an Earthly hell for all his days on account of his grievous actions. We can strip from this man Claudius the fruits of his wicked ambition for the crime of the wanton slaying in cold blood his very own brother."

Capulet stopped and leaned over to hide his face.

"Again, forgive me. My heart is in the coffin now with the late king, and I must pause 'till it come back to me."

Fade out.

EPISODE 17:

The Verdict

CAPULET'S OFFICE WAS SOMBER, FEARFUL. The light was dim. Capulet and his men sat at the large oak table where they had toiled for many months. They waited in this cold darkness, as they had waited for more than a week. Hamlet would not stop fidgeting.

"What now?" Hamlet asked.

"The longer we wait, the better. No need to worry now," Capulet said. They had had this conversation every day since trial ended and Capulet always offered the same words of reassurance.

"What are our chances?" Hamlet asked. Capulet pulled Hamlet and Shakespeare away from the others, into a darker corner of the room where the rest of the team could not hear. "My chances?" he asked again.

"Fifty-fifty," Capulet answered. "Everything is fifty-fifty. There is no need to worry, because the jury will return a verdict either for us or against us. So it's fifty-fifty, like a coin toss."

"That makes no sense," Hamlet said.

"It does make sense in a manner," Capulet argued. "But either way, 'tis out of our hands now. We've done our best. You've performed well, as did your father. And for our part, we put forward the better case. 'Tis up to the hearts of those Danes arrayed for jury."

"If we win, know that I am eternally in your debt. And to you, Billy."

"The reverse holds as true, Friend Hamlet," Capulet said.

"And if we lose?" Hamlet asked. "Do we appeal?"

"Doubtful. All our evidence was admitted, so there shall not be solid footing for appeal. Nor, truth be told, is it clear to what justicial body we would appeal. Indeed, I'm a bit surprised that we've managed to push this matter to trial at all—but we'd all be better off not thinking too much on the matter of jurisdiction. We could, I suppose, push appeal on account of the psychologist's report—about which I'd preferred to have been made aware prior to trial. I'd say that, if we lose, your best bet is to raise an army, march on Elsinore, and exact your mortal revenge at swordpoint."

"Had hoped it wouldn't come to that," Hamlet said.

"Yes. That's why we're here," Capulet said. He gazed away from Hamlet for a moment, his face taking on the dour aspect of a Welsh barrister. "We barristers are, for good or for ill, the last resort before the justice of the blade."

"You know," Hamlet said, "now that you've really, you know, *put that out there*, I suppose I could muster a few thousand troops. You know, if I had to? It's what my father would have done. And my father's father. And my father's father's father. And likely *his* father, as well, though his father's father was a notorious pacifist."

"Yes. 'Twas always thus," Capulet added.

"And, you know, just throwing this out there—had I pressed my claim in the military fashion, I wouldn't have had to pony up so many legal fees."

"Well, well...I..uh..." Capulet coughed. "Well think of the savings! We're really a *value-added* practice, Prince Hamlet. Think of the dubloons that you've saved by not feeding troops, stabling ponies. Spear sharpening costs would have set you back a penny or two, I'd expect."

Hamlet did not look at all persuaded by this line of reasoning. Both Capulet and Billy shifted uneasily, first to the right and then to the left. But, thankfully, fate would save them from diving into a more in-depth justification of their legal fees.

Just then there was powerful knock at the door. They each knew that knock. It would be Montjoy, sent by the King to offer terms of settlement again. Shakespeare went to the door and let the herald in.

"Lord Capulet, 'tis Montjoy to see you," Shakespeare said.

"Who hath sent thee now?"

"The constable of the Court, Sir, on charge from Claudius," Montjoy answered. "Claudius bids me offer settlement upon these terms." Montjoy produced a piece of paper from his pocket and read from it exactly as it was written. "Twenty thousand krone, payable to Hamlet in ten yearly installments, without interest, of course, which is forbidden among good gentiles."

Capulet heard the offer and looked to Hamlet, who shook his head in disagreement. Capulet then looked to Shakespeare, who also shook his head.

"I pray thee bid my former answer back," Capulet said. "Come thou no more for settlement, gentle herald: they shall have none, I swear, but by the verdict; which, if they have as I shall leave 'em them, shall yield them little. Tell the constable."

"I shall, *Lord* Capulet," Montjoy said. He folded the paper and pressed it back into his pocket. "And so fare thee well. Thou never shalt hear herald no more."

None in attendance spoke after Montjoy left the room.

The screen fades out and fades back in on the courtroom at The Hague.[25] The judge says, "Have you good Christian men of the jury reached a verdict?"

"Yup, sure did," the foreman stood and announced. The foreman stood and adjusted the waist of his pants. "We good Christian men of the jury find King Claudius guilty...."

"Liable," the judge interrupted. "Liable, but not guilty. This is a civil matter."

"Whatever," the foreman said. "Whatever you fuckers wanna call it. He did it. Dudn't matter what you call it. We award Denmark to Prince Hamlet."

Capulet and Shakespeare wept, embraced, and then got very drunk.

---

[25] **Editor's Note:** Here, the director took quite a liberty—especially given the state of copyright law in the future. When the screen fades back in at The Hague, the director inserted the unmistakable "gong gong" from *Law and Order*. It seems to me that appropriation of that signature sound from *Law and Order* would almost certainly be a copyright violation. Unless, I suppose, the documentary *Shakespeare! UNWRITTEN!* would fall into some sort of copyright loophole, like, oh, satire or parody.

ACT V

EPISODE 18:

Annie's Song

ANNE SHAKESPEARE EXITED THROUGH THE GARDEN of her London home, from which she had barred the film crew's entrance.[26] Two years had passed since the court at The Hague had delivered their verdict—a unanimous verdict in favor of Prince Hamlet. She smiled broadly at the camera and blushed. She wore very fine clothing, of gilded silk of the type that only the richest of women would wear. Her voice was clear and energetic. She began:

"Now is the winter of our discontent made glorious summer by this secret son of Wales. We are happy, at long last. Our recent

---

[26] **Editor's Note:** This episode 17 is alone among the episodes of *SHAKESPEARE! Unwritten!* in that it contains only a single, long soliloquy. This came as a surprise to my team of interns, all of who associated Shakespeare with long soliloquies. Annie is the only person who appears in real-time in this episode; she delivers her soliloquy sometimes directly to the camera as she walks along the street in her London neighborhood, and sometimes over montages of pictures the film crew had captured during their time in the 16th Century. It's odd, given the director's stated opposition to the misogyny inherent in 16th Century culture, that this episode is the only one that features Anne so prominently. It is doubly odd, given the content of Anne's soliloquy. One would think that, upon learning of the true author of Shakespeare's plays, the director would have focused *on that author*. Well, I suppose that the more things change, the more things stay the same. It's a shame, really.

success came upon us so swift, so severe, that I am so often reduced to laughter. London Society quite loves our Billy Shakespeare, and we've fixed ourselves proper among them. Society ladies here joke with me. "Annie," they say, "Will'am is so homely, how did he ever win your heart?" They speak in jest, of course, but I can't but answer them true. 'Twas his sonnets, I say.

I feel a fool now when I think back on those days in Swansea. I was so young. He was so young and so strong. O, how my heart beat out of my chest as I ran full-throated across the valley for a secret meeting with my lover. And he was my lover, though he never touched me. His face near black, and his hands, when he crawled out of the mines of an evening; his skin covered in soot and noxious poisons. His touch would have been the death of me for all the poisons of the coal mines. Still, I begged: Touch me, I begged him, touch me! But he would not relent. Because he could not touch me—and because he could not kiss me—he wrote to me.

"Shall I compare thee to a summer's day?" he asked. "Thou art more lovely and more temperate." My God, did I love him. He made me the most beautiful woman in a world of promise. He made me feel that I was, anyway. So it was his poetry that won my heart.

This is the misunderstanding of certain men of ambition. They believe that a woman's heart is to be bought, or won through trickery, with great lavish gifts of gold and feats of heraldry. But they are at least in me mistaken in this belief. I believe myself to be a noble and true woman, if somewhat strong-willed. And the true heart of this noble woman was won much more cheaply, with only a few rhyming couplets spoken truthfully. For Billy was a true poet.

And then the hard times. For five long years was I imprisoned in that flat in Stratford-upon-Avon, just a plaything stored away from the world, whiling away day after silent stupid day in endless patient waiting. Endless patient waiting for the "master" of the house to return home from his day of duties so that I might perform my modest wifely duties. Waiting. Waiting. Wondering when it would be my turn to have a guiding hand in my life's own virtue. And do not hear me wrong, Billy was always as kind and just with me as any man who has ever lived was to the woman he loved. But he was all I had in the world—my whole world was devoted to waiting, to waiting, to waiting for him. How could any woman so positioned think herself other than property?

I confess it now, even to my dear husband, that when I removed myself to London I had it in my mind that Billy would not follow me. His case in Belgium, or wherever it was, whether pushed to successful consummation or failure, would bring him back to Birmingham with eyes set only on the next case and twenty years hence I would see him become Lord Shakespeare of Shakespeare & Capulet Barristers—for all of his weaknesses, he was a strong and ambitious man. But in a world so arranged, no strength and no ambition can put straight what has been made crooked between lovers.

Or so I thought.

While laboring away on that Hamlet case, and my love Billy did labor through the days and through the nights, he stole himself away at every chance with a quill and paper and he wrote to me. His poetry. Perhaps the only way he ever spoke truly to anyone. Perhaps the only way anyone has ever spoken truly.

Canst thou, O cruel, say I love thee not,

When I against myself with thee partake?

Do I not think on thee, when I forgot

Am of myself, all tyrant for thy sake?

Who hateth thee that I do call my friend?

On whom frown'st thou that I do fawn upon?

Nay, if thou lour'st on me, do I not spend

Revenge upon myself with present moan?

What merit do I in myself respect

That is so proud thy service to despise,

When all my best doth worship thy defect,

Commanded by the motion of thine eyes?

  But love, hate on, for now I know thy mind;

  Those that can see, thou lov'st, and I am blind.

Who could not love that poet? Who could not love this man?

It was here in London that I turned then to his plays—those works he'd labor'd and scribbled upon all those days in Stratford-upon-Avon. I had nowt to do but await out our pregnancy, which I suppose I should mention that I saw through to completion and brought forth a lovely child. So with nothing to do, and on orders of bed rest, I read Billy's plays. In my boredom, well...I wouldn't say I 're-wrote' them. But I took a pretty heavy hand in editing them.

It's not that they were bad, *per se*, although bits of them were quite awful. There were some good themes, some cute turns of phrases that he'd picked up here and there. They weren't bad, but they certainly weren't very good. And, truthfully, they were terribly boring. He was all into *theatre verite* at the time and the realist movement. Speaking frankly, who wants to watch a play about the day-to-day goings on of a barrister's office in Birmingham? No, me neither.

Theatre was never his true calling, anyway. And, theatre is a passing thing. It's hardly a vocation for a man of ambition like my Billy. Think of all our stories that we love so much, handed down for hundreds of generations over thousands of years. No one remembers who wrote them or the actors who played them. We remember the *stories*. Truth be told, I mostly just re-wrote a few thousand-year old stories with Billy's words. For although my Billy doesn't have a very good handle on plot or character development, he is quite a wordsmith.

He's off at our Globe Theatre right now engaged in the direction of one of "his" plays, *Richard Three*. Which he'd originally titled *"My Stupid Boss, the Cripple"*. I'm certain it will open to fanfare and a packed house as all of "his" plays do.

It is a point of pride for me, though, that "his" plays have brought us such fame. For along with that fame has come renewed fervor and interest in his earlier work, his sonnets. And now, the very same sonnets that won my heart are recited, lover to lover, in pubs across the land and in secret trysts in wooded groves just beyond pleasant meadows. 'Tis with his words that the tongue-tied groom addresses his waiting bride; 'tis with his incantations does the merry bridesmaid bless such union. And, 'tis with his lamentations that this nation remembers our lovers long since consigned to their eternal commissions. 'Tis an irony, I suppose, that in my clandestine labors and secret machinations against the patriarchy, as it were, I have won not my own fame, but rather have secured eternally, from this day to the ending of the world, the legacy of the first and greatest poet of the English language, my husband, the Bard of Stratford-upon-Avon.

Well, enough of me. I'm off to our Globe Theatre. My most trusted maidservant tells me that a surprise visitor does approach. Be well, Everyone. Pip pip.

EPISODE 19:

Now Is the Winter of Our Discontent

THE GLOBE THEATRE STAGE STOOD EMPTY. The hall was quiet and dark until a single light shone down from rafters and illuminated a single spot on the stage. Then, softly, a man named Burbage limped out into the spotlight. He wore thick makeup to make his 35-year-old face appear ancient; he exaggerated his false limp, and the left side of his face was contorted. He wore a massive lump of cloth on his right shoulder to mock a hunchback.

"Now is the winter of our discontent made glorious summer by this son of York," Burbage moaned. The words were so slurred that none could understand them. "The clouds that lou'rd upon our house in the deep bosom of the ocean, buried. Now are our brows...."

"CUT! CUT! No, no, no, no!" Shakespeare shouted. He stormed out from stage right and light came upon the stage. "This is all wrong! We've been over this a thousand time, Ricky. He's not mentally deficient, he's just got a bit of a limp."

"Sorry, Sir," Burbage mumbled. His affected limp and slurred speech now disappeared. "Thought I'd just really go for it once and see how it felt. Really put myself out there, you know?"

Shakespeare saw something moving off of stage left. He held up his hand to quiet Burbage, and then took a step toward stage left.

"Do my eyes deceive me? Is it not the man himself, Lord Capulet, come to call on his old esquire?"

Charles Ap Ulet entered from stage left. He had grown older in the two years that had passed since the Hamlet trial. But he now walked tall, with no limp. His left hand swung in locomotion at his side.

"Little Boddy Shakes!"

"What is this I see before me?" Shakespeare asked. He smiled from ear to ear and rushed to embrace his former employer. "Speak, Sir, and explain yourself. Why do you now stand so erect?"

They clasped hands and half-hugged at the center of the stage. The limelight now off of Burbage and onto the old law buddies.

"Oh, this? Experimental surgery, Will. Chap down in Paris set me right straight. Knocked me about a bit, tied me up a while, soon enough I'm right as rain!"

"What kind of French magician? Be he devil or angel?"

"No, no, Will. Not sorcery at all. They call it skeeeance, or something quite similar. No, quite different than sorcery, I'm afraid. Turns out that my back was not possessed by a demon, as my barbers had previously surmised, but in fact I had a mild case of what they call *scoliosis*."

Shakespeare then turned to Burbage, hiding near the edge of the stage, and he shouted:

"Scoliosis, you say? Hear that, Burbage? He's not had a stroke, he's just got scoliosis. Get your head out and keep up with the times.

Off with ye!" He turned back to Capulet. "But you do look right as rain, Sir. Bet your quality of life has seen mark'd improvement."

"Yes, to be certain. Wife's quite happier, too, which goes without saying. Although, I admit, I am from time to time forlorn regarding the many decades wasted in abbey praying Jesus to foreclose on the Devil's homestead within my spine. Still, better late than never, eh Will?"

"I'd say so, Lord Capulet."

"Oh, none of that Lord Capulet business. You're no longer in my employ, Bill. Although, speaking technically, my recent knighthood obligates you to address me as *Sir* Charles Ap Ulet, I'm just simple Charles Ap Ulet, now to you. Call me Chuck."

"Yes, Sir, Chuck, Sir! Knighthood, eh?"

"Yes, Billy. Cost me quite a farthing, or quite a shilling, or a pound, or what have you. Contribution to the Queen's re-coronation fund."

"What business brings you here to London to my humble playhouse?"

Charles Ap Ulet ambled in small circles around the stage, rejoicing in his newfound ability to walk. He smiled as he spoke and as he made circles around William Shakespeare.

"Wife and I just back from a tour of the continent and, of course, my recent convalescence among the gentry of gay Paris. When I heard tell of Shakespeare's Globe Theatre I told my wife, 'Sharon! We must stop by and see my old charge, that hungry bastard Boddy Shakes.' Can't stay long I'm afraid."

"No? 'Tis a pity. We open tonight. *Richard Three*. Would love for you to see it."

"*Richard Three?* Uh. Would I have had to see the first two to understand what goes on?"

"Couldn't hurt, of course, but it's a stand-alone piece, as well. We're sold out, of course...but I could secure your entry into my personal box seats. Annie will be there and she'd love to see you."

"I cannot, alas. We've booked passage already and I'm afraid we're a bit behind schedule as it is. And, anyway, my dreams never lay in the cheap seats, Will. I was a born performer."

"You could read for Gloucester! Burbage is making a hash of it."

"No. 'Tis far too late for that in my life. My physical deformity did foreclose that vocation to me many decades ago, Will, and now I must confess that after our present voyage home I must make a far more sinister fare."

"Sir?"

"Dying, Will. As all men must. The surgeon in Paris fixed me right as rain, but tells me that I have a tumor internal. Won't be long at all for me, in fact."

"Stay in London, Sir. We've a whole season of performances right round the corner. Could find you any number of roles. I owe you that, if nothing else. That day in your office when you confessed to me your love of the theatre, I did cry out for you, Sir. And all this you see—all—all opportunity afforded to me by your faith in me in the matter of Hamlet. Stay, Charles. Stay here, with me, on this stage."

"Nonsense, Will. All the world's a stage, and all the men and women merely players; they have their exits and their entrances. No. I've lived my dream already—not the dream I intended, of course, but a dream still. Good friends, loving wife, successful career. I can't complain. No, Will, it's not time for my entry onto your stage. 'Tis time for my exit."

"Back to Birmingham, Charles?"

"Birmingham? God's peace, I wouldn't return to that dungeon for all the hats in France. It's awfully dreary there. And the English are a dour people, after all, aren't they, Will?"

"They are that, Sir."

"Yes, dour. None of the vivaciousness, none of the vitality of we Welsh. But you can't blame them—the food is awful, the weather is awful, and they've no sense of romance. No, for me it's time to ready myself for my final exit. And I'll do it as I always wanted, leaping and running through orchards of ripe fruit and fields of hay. I'm going home, Will. To Wales."

"To Wales?"

"Should God and St. David protect us all, perhaps, by grace, I shall live long enough to see you return home as well," Capulet said.

"Perhaps, Sir."

"Yes, well, I'm off then. To Wales."

"To Wales, Sir. To Wales."

FIN

AFTERWORD

There you have it: the true story of Shakespeare's life and, at long last, the truth of the authorship of Shakespeare's plays. It's shocking stuff.

But what does this revelation *mean* for our contemporary world? How does it alter our perception of Shakespeare to know that credit for Shakespeare's legacy should be borne not by our noble hero, but by his heavy-handed editor, his wife Anne? I don't have the answer to those questions and neither do my interns. We approached this project knowing that it would not fall on our humble team to provide these answers. Our charge in this matter was simply to report and to let our readers decide. Regardless, the *idea* of Shakespeare is now so strongly set in our collective memory that even the revelation of actual, real documentary footage from the future/past won't change the hearts or minds of most Shakespeare fans. In the end, *SHAKESPEARE! Unwritten!* and this adaptation of it are...well...they are full of sound and fury, but signifying nothing.

And, anyway, I've moved on. Don't get me wrong: I feel honored to have played a part in finally elevating Anne Shakespeare to her rightful place in history. But now I'm all about this other item that we found, THE AUTHORIZED TRUE AND COMPLETELY RELIABLE HISTORY OF WESTERN CIVILIZATION. Remember in *Back to the Future*, when Biff gets a hold of that Gray's Sports Almanac? And then he basically can just do whatever he wants because he knows the future? That's kind of how I feel right now, because the stuff in this *AUTHORIZED TRUE AND COMPLETELY RELIABLE HISTORY OF WESTERN CIVILIZATION* is fascinating.

You won't believe what happens in 2019!

About the Author

Tyler Coulson was born in rural Illinois. He graduated with distinction from the University of Iowa College of Law and practiced in the corporate reorganization group of a leading international firm in Chicago. In 2011, he walked across the United States with his dog, Mabel. He lives in Chicago.

Other Titles

Check out these other great titles by Tyler Coulson:

BY MEN OR BY THE EARTH. The incredible story of Coulson's 2011 walk across America with his dog. It is the story of how and why he set out to walk across North America and of what he learned along the way. Part memoir, part revelation, part self-criticism, part instruction manual—Coulson's account is a brutally honest, depiction of a flawed man struggling to survive in a flawed system, and of the unshakeable bond between a man and his dog.

ATTORNEYS AFTER THE CRASH. Seductive, appalling, romantic, and revolting: On September 15, 2008, fourteen attorneys are stranded in the mountains after a plane crash. One survivor, Neal, tests the limits of his resolve and of his morality in order to survive as he slowly becomes trapped among corpses in the wreckage of the plane. He struggles to survive and to find meaning in an amoral world, all while toiling at his last assignment as an attorney for his grotesque boss: The Catalog of the Dead. *Attorneys After the Crash* is the definitive fictional characterization of sociopathic tendencies in the American legal system.